The Forsyte

CW00503191

A play by

Pat and Derek Hoddinott

Dramatized from the novels by John Galsworthy

Samuel French – London
New York – Toronto – Hollywood

© 1991 BY PAT AND DEREK HODDINOTT

Rights of Performance by Amateurs are controlled by Samuel French Ltd, 52 Fitzroy Street, London W1P 6JR, and they, or their authorized agents, issue licences to amateurs on payment of a fee. **It is an infringement of the Copyright to give any performance or public reading of the play before the fee has been paid and the licence issued.**

The Royalty Fee indicated below is subject to contract and subject to variation at the sole discretion of Samuel French Ltd.

Basic fee for each and every performance by amateurs in the British Isles	Code M

The Professional Rights in this play are controlled by ERIC GLASS LTD, 28 Berkeley Square, London W1X 6HD.

The publication of this play does not imply that it is necessarily available for performance by amateurs or professionals, either in the British Isles or Overseas. Amateurs and professionals considering a production are strongly advised in their own interests to apply to appropriate agents for consent before starting rehearsals or booking a theatre or hall.

The play is a dramatization of three of the novels of John Galsworthy: *The Man of Property, In Chancery,* and *To Let*.

ISBN 0 573 01766 2

Please see page viii for further copyright information.

THE FORSYTE SAGA

First produced at the Salisbury Playhouse on 16th February, 1989, prior to a national tour of Great Britain, which began on 10th January, 1991, at the Haymarket Theatre, Basingstoke, produced by Mark Furness Ltd and John Newman for Newpalm Productions, in association with the Horseshoe Theatre Company, Basingstoke.

Irene	Nyree Dawn Porter
Soames	Philip Madoc
Philip Bosinney	Barry Quin
June	Harriet Benson
James	Oliver Bradshaw
Aunt Juley	Beryl King
Aunt Hester	Joyce Fenby
Servant	Simon Hewitt
Young Jolyon	William Whymper
Annette	Gina Cameron
Fleur	Sharon Small
Michael Mont	Simon Hewitt
Jon	Jeffrey Harmer
Maid	Harriet Benson

Directed by Adrian Reynolds
Designed by Stephen Howell
Lighting by Raymond Cross
Costumes by Elroy Ashmore

CHARACTERS

Soames, a man of property; born 1855
Irene, his wife; born 1863
James, his father; born 1811
Juley, his aunt; born 1814
Hester, his aunt; born 1815
Annette, his second wife; born 1880
Fleur, his daughter by his marriage to Annette; born 1901
Philip Bosinney, an architect
Young Jo, son of Old Jolyon; born 1847
June, Young Jo's daughter by his first marriage; born 1869
Jon, Young Jo's son by his marriage to Irene; born 1901
Michael Mont, Fleur's suitor
Servant
Maid

(If required, the following parts may be doubled: **Bosinney/Jon, June/Fleur, Mont/Servant.**)

The action of the play takes place at Old Jolyon's house in Stanhope Gate; Soames's house in Knightsbridge; the botanical gardens; Bosinney's rooms; June's art gallery in Cork Street; Holly's house in the country and Young Jo's house at Robin Hill, Richmond

Time—between the years 1886 and 1920

SYNOPSIS OF SCENES

ACT I

Scene 1	Old Jolyon's house at Stanhope Gate. 1886
Scene 2	Soames's house in Knightsbridge. Four weeks later
Scene 3	The same. Several months later, 1887.
Scene 4	The same. A week later
Scene 5	The Botanical Gardens. The following day
Scene 6	Soames's house in Knightsbridge. Several days later
Scene 7	The same. A few weeks later
Scene 8	The same. Several weeks later
Scene 9	Bosinney's rooms. Later the same day
Scene 10	Soames's house in Knightsbridge. An hour later
Scene 11	The same. Twelve years later, 1899

ACT II

Scene 1	Soames's house in Knightsbridge. January 1901
Scene 2	June's art gallery in Cork Street. May, 1920
Scene 3	Jo's and Irene's house at Robin Hill, Richmond. Later the same day
Scene 4	Holly's house in the country. A week later
Scene 5	Soames's house in Knightsbridge. Three weeks later
Scene 6	Jo's and Irene's house at Robin Hill, Richmond. Several weeks later
Scene 7	The same. A few weeks later
Scene 8	Soames's house in Knightsbridge. A few weeks later
Scene 9	Jo's and Irene's house at Robin Hill, Richmond. Several weeks later
Scene 10	The same. Two weeks later
Scene 11	Soames's house in Knightsbridge. Three months later

Act II

Photograph of the Salisbury Playhouse production by Peter Brown

PRODUCTION NOTE

Amateur groups, even those with limited resources, should not be daunted by the word "Saga" in the title and believe such a play is large in scope and therefore outside their range.

If necessary this play could be played to decorative curtains, provided exits and entrances and the three distinct playing areas are clearly indicated by their positioning and lighting.

Also, there are few demands on furniture (two small cane tables, four cane chairs and one small cane settee) and props (just crockery, glasses and trays) to inhibit even the smallest of societies with the smallest stages on which to perform.

Indeed, such simplicity allows more scope for costumes and wigs, an important element of the production, covering the thirty-five years during which the action takes place.

Pat and Derek Hoddinott

COPYRIGHT INFORMATION

(See also page ii)

This play is fully protected under the Copyright Laws of the British Commonwealth of Nations, the United States of America and all countries of the Berne and Universal Copyright Conventions.

All rights, including Stage, Motion Picture, Radio, Television, Public Reading, and Translation into Foreign Languages, are strictly reserved.

No part of this publication may lawfully be reproduced in ANY form or by any means—photocopying, typescript, recording (including video-recording), manuscript, electronic, mechanical, or otherwise—or be transmitted or stored in a retrieval system, without prior permission.

Licences for amateur performances are issued subject to the understanding that it shall be made clear in all advertising matter that the audience will witness an amateur performance; that the names of the authors of the plays shall be included on all announcements and on all programmes; and that the integrity of the authors' work will be preserved.

The Royalty Fee is subject to contract and subject to variation at the sole discretion of Samuel French Ltd.

In Theatres or Halls seating Six Hundred or more the fee will be subject to negotiation.

In Territories Overseas the fee quoted in this Acting Edition may not apply. A fee will be quoted on application to our local authorized agent, or if there is no such agent, on application to Samuel French Ltd, London.

VIDEO RECORDING OF AMATEUR PRODUCTIONS

Please note that the copyright laws governing video-recording are extremely complex and that it should not be assumed that any play may be video-recorded *for whatever purpose* without first obtaining the permission of the appropriate agents. That fact that a play is published by Samuel French Ltd does not indicate that video rights are available or that Samuel French Ltd controls such rights.

Other plays by Derek Hoddinott
published by Samuel French Ltd

Din-Dins
Hello and Goodbye
The Little Photographer
(from the story by Daphne du Maurier)

ACT I

Scene 1

Old Jolyon's house at Stanhope Gate. 1886

The set suggests a Victorian conservatory much favoured of the times, though to the individuals concerned, it could also suggest a prison in which all the Forsytes and their ilk are trapped—by convention and the need to hide their inner emotions from the outside world

There are three exits: R, L *and* C. *There are two cane tables with chairs* R *and* L, *and* C *there is a cane settee which, in Act II, is replaced by a circular seat similar to that used around the base of a tree. A selection of indoor plants—palms, aspidistras, ferns, etc.—are gathered in the corners upstage*

It is within this area that the drama is played out. To clarify the locations it might help if R *is identified as Soames's Knightsbridge house and* L *as the Robin Hill home of Irene and Jo. Other locations can be placed* C

As the CURTAIN *rises we discover a tableau of the Forsytes down* C *celebrating the engagement of June Forsyte, aged seventeen, and Philip Bosinney, in his twenties. Also present are James, aged seventy-five, Soames, aged thirty-one, Irene, aged twenty-three, and Aunts Hester and Juley, aged seventy-one and seventy-two respectively. A Servant waits upon them*

As the Lights come up full, James raises his glass of champagne in a toast

James ... so it is with great pleasure that I ask you to raise your glasses and drink a toast to June and Philip.
All (*raising their glasses*) June and Philip.

They all drink, after which there is gentle clapping. Then they break into two groups: the Aunts, James and Soames, and Irene, Bosinney (*to whom she is obviously attracted*) *and June. After the toast the Servant moves around replenishing the glasses*

James (*moving to the Aunts*) I have to say it! I don't like the man!
Aunt Hester James! He'll hear you.
James Don't care if he does, Hester. I can say what I please. After all, I *am* head of this family.
Aunt Hester That doesn't give you the right to spoil June's day.
Aunt Juley The buccaneer!
James What's that, Juley?
Aunt Juley My pet name for him. The buccaneer!
James What's she talking about, Hester?
Aunt Juley Shall I tell him, Hester?

Aunt Hester No dear, but you're going to anyway.
Aunt Juley Well, James, when we first met Mr Bosinney he was wearing this peculiar hat . . .
James Peculiar hat?
Aunt Juley It appeared as if someone had just sat on it making it look rather like a pirate's hat. And he actually wore it like that! To be different, I suppose. Hence the name: the buccaneer. Anyway, the really funny thing was he put it down on a nearby chair and when Hester came to sit down—well you know how bad her eyesight is?

Hester sighs irritably at this

She tried to shoo it away, thinking it was a stray cat.

James and Juley laugh and then go into animated conversation as Hester looks on with disdain

June Tell me, Irene, as my closest friend what do you *really* think of him?
Bosinney Good Lord, June! You make me sound like a racehorse. You'll want to examine my teeth next!

They laugh

Soames They tell me, Bosinney, you show promise as an architect?
June He's going to be a great architect one day, Uncle Soames. Aren't you, my darling? (*She kisses Bosinney on the cheek affectionately*)
Bosinney If the reports you hear, sir, are as good as June's estimation of me, then I'll be rich in no time.
Soames It's not only a talent for making money that counts, Bosinney. It's the hard work that goes with it. Am I not right, Irene?
Irene (*smiling coldly*) Yes, Soames. You're right—as always.

The sarcasm is not lost on Soames

June You didn't answer my question, Irene.
Irene What question was that, June?
June What do you think of my fiancé?
Bosinney Please, June. You're embarrassing Mrs Forsyte.
June Don't be silly, Phil. Irene's my greatest chum. We haven't any secrets from one another, have we?

June smiles at Irene who returns it. June takes Bosinney's arm as Soames moves downstage to the Aunts

By the way, my darling. I think it's time you made a speech.
Bosinney Oh, no . . .
June Oh, yes. What do you think, Irene? Shouldn't he make a speech?
Irene It *is* the done thing. The family will expect it . . .
June (*excitedly*) Come along, Phil.
Bosinney (*resisting*) No! Please . . .

Irene laughs gaily as June begins to drag Bosinney downstage C

(*Looking back at Irene*) How could you do this to me?

June (*to all*) Everyone! Please! Listen!

Everyone stops talking and looks at June

Phil is going to make a speech.

Aunt Juley Oh, Lord! Not another one!

James I don't know what you mean by that, Juley.

Bosinney (*clearing his throat*) Er ... it appears I'm required to say a few words——

Juley The fewer the better, young man!

Aunt Hester Juley!

Bosinney (*smiling*)—though I must confess that June, (*he looks at her lovingly*) dear June, is much better equipped than I for such a task.

James That's because she's a Forsyte, young man.

Aunt Juley Well said, James. Well said.

Bosinney As you say, sir, June is a Forsyte and for someone like myself the prospect of becoming a member of such an illustrious family is daunting indeed. However, I hope to acquit myself to the best of my ability and in so doing try to live up to the traditions and high standards the Forsytes have set for themselves.

Some "hear, hear"s from James and Juley

Well ... that's all I have to say really ...

There is an awkward silence for a brief moment and then Irene begins to clap somewhat enthusiastically, so encouraging everyone else to join in. Bosinney smiles with relief at Irene as he moves towards her. June moves to James and the Aunts, who begin talking amongst themselves

Thank you.

Irene What for?

Bosinney For rescuing me.

Irene (*smiling*) They are rather frightening, aren't they? The Forsytes.

Bosinney (*surprised at her honesty*) Er ... yes I suppose they are. When they're all together like this one feels so much the outsider.

Irene Yes.

Bosinney You felt like that too? At the beginning?

Irene One feels like that now ... (*Realizing what she has said*) Oh, please ... I shouldn't have spoken like that. (*Beat*) I've never said anything like that to anyone before.

Bosinney You honour me.

Irene In what way?

Bosinney In confiding in me.

Irene It wasn't a confidence. It was merely a slip of the tongue.

Bosinney (*smiling*) Still, I will not betray your sentiment whether it be the slip of the tongue or not, Mrs Forsyte.

Irene looks at him directly and likes what she sees

Irene (*smiling*) If we're to be related at some future date I think perhaps we should dispense with the formalities ... Don't you?

Bosinney looks directly at her, too. A charge is ignited between them

Bosinney Yes ... yes, I agree.
Irene Then ... Philip, I have to tell you ...
Bosinney Yes, Irene?
Irene That you're staring at me.
Bosinney (*not batting an eyelid*) Yes, I know.
Irene (*looking away with some amusement*) You seem to have overcome your feeling of being an outsider ...

During the following, June moves from James and the Aunts to Bosinney and Irene

Bosinney That's because, at this precise moment, all the Forsytes—with the exception of you—have ceased to exist.

On joining them, June takes Bosinney's arm and kisses his cheek

June I do hope you two will be good friends.
Irene Why shouldn't we be?
Bosinney What a funny thing you are, June. (*He kisses her hand*)
Irene If it makes you feel any better, June, I think Philip is utterly charming and, I suspect, very, very talented.

They go into animated conversation

James (*looking at them*) For the life of me I don't know what June sees in him.
Aunt Hester They're in love, James.
James They've no business to be! Fashionable nonsense!
Soames I hear he's a promising architect.
James With no commissions.
Aunt Hester (*trying to be kind*) I ... er ... think he has, one ... (*she shrugs*) possibly.
James I wouldn't know, Hester. No-one ever tells me anything.
Soames Now, now, Father.
James I'm going to get myself some more bubbly.

James goes to the Servant nearby and replenishes his glass during the following

Aunt Juley I must say I'm surprised at Old Jolyon allowing this engagement.
Soames Where is he by the way?
Aunt Hester Where most of the male Forsytes congregate at times like these. In the smoking-room discussing business and the latest share prices. I'm surprised you and your father aren't with them, Soames.
Aunt Juley They tell me there's no chance of their getting married for years. Bosinney hasn't a penny.
Soames Really?
Aunt Juley Do you mean to say you didn't know, Soames?
Soames Know what, Aunt? I'm only interested in facts, not gossip. Excuse me ...

Soames moves away to join James

Aunt Juley Soames can be so cutting at times, can't he?

Suddenly, Irene starts to laugh at something Bosinney has said. They are close together so effectively cutting June out of their group. Soames stares at Irene, not listening to James

Aunt Hester Irene seems to be enjoying herself.
Aunt Juley She always does when Soames isn't by her side.
Aunt Hester I do hear they don't get on.
Aunt Juley You heard that, too? Soames is a cold fish by all accounts.
Aunt Hester (*moving closer to Juley*) I did overhear once ... Mind you, I wasn't listening deliberately, you understand ...
Aunt Juley Of course not, dear.
Aunt Hester That Irene had asked for separate rooms.
Aunt Juley No!
Aunt Hester Yes. I fear so.
Aunt Juley Well, that confirms what I heard a few weeks ago.
Aunt Hester You heard something too then, dear?
Aunt Juley That Soames is ... difficult with women.
Aunt Hester (*thinking about it*) Difficult? Really? Well, Soames has always been reserved.
Aunt Juley That's as maybe. I still say Irene's too pretty for her own good.
Aunt Hester What was her father? I forget.
Aunt Juley A Heron.
Aunt Hester A what?
Aunt Juley Professor Heron.
Aunt Hester Oh, no money in that, of course.

During the following, Soames leaves James and moves to Irene. When he reaches her he takes her arm and leads her downstage

Aunt Juley They say her mother's father was cement or something of the sort.
Aunt Hester Really?
Aunt Juley It didn't make any difference though. He still went bankrupt!
Aunt Hester Oh.
Aunt Juley No. Soames will have trouble with that one. You mark my words. He'll have trouble.
Soames (*very low*) What do you think you're doing?
Irene I don't understand.
Soames You understand perfectly.
Irene You mean I was laughing? I appeared to be enjoying myself? Is that what you mean, Soames?
Soames The only thing you appear to be is cheap, my dear.
Irene And you don't possess anything cheap, do you, Soames?
Soames There is a standard of behaviour expected of us. Remember who you are.
Irene (*hissing*) I do! Constantly!!

Soames Please. Not here.

Irene No, we mustn't show the cracks in the façade, must we?

Soames If we had been here longer I'd have blamed the champagne for your behaviour.

Irene Behaviour? What behaviour? I'm talking to my best friend's fiancé. You wish me to ignore him?

Soames I wish you to stop staring at him as if . . . (*He stops himself*)

Irene As if what, Soames?

Soames Don't provoke me, Irene. It's unseemly. This is an important family occasion and the least I expect from my wife . . .

Irene Don't call me that!

Soames Why not? You are.

Irene In name only.

Soames That, as you well know, madam, is not of my choosing. You know what I want from you, Irene.

Irene And you know what I *demand* from you, Soames. (*Close to him*) Freedom!!

Irene moves upstage to Bosinney leaving Soames looking embarrassed and sipping his champagne. He slowly moves towards James as Irene joins Bosinney and they talk animatedly making June feel left out once more. She drifts away towards the Aunts during the following

Aunt Hester I'd like some more champagne.

Aunt Juley Don't you think you've had enough?

Aunt Hester Don't be silly, Juley. One never has enough of champagne. (*Peering around her*) Where *is* the servant.

Aunt Juley (*beckoning the Servant to approach*) I do wish you'd do something about your eyesight, Hester. It's getting worse.

Aunt Hester There's nothing wrong with my eyesight so I'd appreciate it if you wouldn't keep on about it.

June joins them

Aunt Juley Ah, June my dear.

Aunt Hester How could you bear to tear yourself away from that handsome young man of yours?

Aunt Juley Except he doesn't seem to be quite "yours" at the moment, does he, my dear?

June They're only talking, Aunt Juley. About architecture.

Aunt Juley (*raising her eyebrows*) Really? I didn't know that was one of Irene's strong points.

Aunt Hester (*rushing in*) I think, June dear, you're going to be terribly happy.

June Do you think so, Aunt?

Aunt Hester Of course. I wish I were young again. The trouble is you don't appreciate your youth until you're our age.

Aunt Juley And when you're our age you're too old to remember it!

June and the Aunts laugh but are eclipsed by the laughter of Irene and Bosinney as they move upstage to the C *entrance. All the others turn and watch*

As the Lights fade to half, piano music plays

The Servant clears the glasses and Soames, Bosinney, Irene, James and the Aunts exit

June moves R *and sits*

Scene 2

Soames's house in Knightsbridge. Four weeks later

As the Lights come up, Irene enters

Irene June darling, I'm sorry to keep you waiting. (*She kisses her cheek*)
June That's all right, Irene. I really came to see Soames. Is he in?
Irene I'm afraid he isn't. He'll be home any minute though.
June I'll wait a few moments if I may.
Irene Of course. Where's Philip?
June I hope he's busy working in his office.
Irene Plenty of commissions then?
June Thanks to Soames, yes. I would have come sooner except that Phil—oh, I could have killed him—kept it all a secret until yesterday. When I heard the news I just had to come round and thank Uncle Soames personally.
Irene I don't understand. What has Soames got to do with it?
June Don't you know?
Irene What should I know, June?
June Robin Hill.
Irene (*shrugging*) I'm sorry.
June Oh, dear, how embarrassing. (*She sighs*) Well, the day after our engagement Soames called at Phil's office to talk about a commission.
Irene Four weeks ago?
June Yes. They even visited the site at Robin Hill together. Afterwards he gave Phil a commission to build a house.
Irene For whom?
June Why . . . you of course!

Irene moves away shattered

I'm sorry. I really thought you knew.
Irene Yes . . .er . . . under normal circumstances no doubt that would be the case.
June (*trying to redeem the situation; smiling*) Of course! It's to be a surprise! And I've spoiled it. Soames will never forgive me.
Irene (*putting on a brave face*) Don't worry, June, I won't say a word! Imagine! I'll be living in a house designed by your husband. Isn't that exciting?
June Phil doesn't stop talking about it. He's already completed masses of drawings. He's had some marvellous ideas.

Irene He's very talented. Didn't I say so?

June Oh, Irene, he's so exciting to be with. I mean I never thought architecture could be so interesting but when Phil talks about porticos, architraves, landscaping, oh, I don't know, he makes it sound like a romantic novel.

They laugh gently together

Irene You really are in love with him, aren't you?

June Yes. Well, you must admit he *is* attractive. Don't you find him attractive, Irene?

Irene June! What an improper question.

June Improper or not I can tell you do. I noticed it at our engagement party. I'm so happy, Irene. And grandfather's been so marvellous about everything.

Irene He'll miss you when you marry.

June Yes, he will, but I've promised to go and see him as often as possible. I only wish my father could have been part of it all.

Irene There's no use looking back at the past, June. Not in this family. If the Forsytes don't approve of anything or anyone then it doesn't exist. Shall I tell you something? I admire your father.

June What?

Irene Not for the hurt he must have caused you in running off the way he did. But for the fact that he didn't care what the rest of the family thought. He must be a very strong man to break out like that.

June You're a bad influence, Irene. I shall be banned from coming here.

They laugh as the door opens

Soames enters

Soames Well . . . well . . . what's all this?

June Hallo, Uncle. (*She goes and kisses his cheek*)

Soames Good-afternoon, June.

Soames moves to Irene and kisses her cheek. She immediately moves away

Irene . . .

Irene Women's talk, that's all.

Soames Women's talk, eh? And what's that?

Irene Idle chatter about weddings, dresses and the like. Nothing that would interest you, Soames.

Soames (*to June*) Wedding? Already?

June (*catching Irene's eye*) Er . . . yes . . .

Soames You and Bosinney planning on a short engagement then?

June Er . . . (*She looks to Irene for help*)

Irene Weddings take a great deal of time and preparation, if they're to do justice to the Forsytes. You should know that.

Soames That's very true. And I suppose not having your mother . . . well . . . Irene will be of great assistance I'm sure. (*Directly to Irene*) It'll give you something to do, won't it, my dear?

June I think I'd better go. (*Going to Irene and kissing her*) Thank you, Irene.
Irene Goodbye, June.
June Goodbye, Uncle Soames.
Soames Goodbye.

As Irene moves with her to the exit, Soames sits

June exits

Irene returns

Come to talk about her lover, I suppose?

Irene doesn't reply

It seems to me she's much sweeter on him that he is on her. She's always following him about, I hear.
Irene (*approaching him*) You've no business to say such a thing.
Soames Why not? Anyone can see it.
Irene No they can't. And if they could it's disgraceful to say so.
Soames You seem quite obsessed with June.
Irene Obsessed? She's my closest friend that's all.
Soames Close friend? The daughter of a renegade! You do well to choose your friends more carefully. And I'll tell you another thing! Now that she has Bosinney in tow she won't care twopence about you and you'll realize it soon enough.
Irene I realize something that affects me more! How little regard you have for me or my feelings.
Soames What do you mean?
Irene As it happens June didn't come to see me today. She came to see you. To thank you for commissioning Philip Bosinney to build us a house at Robin Hill.
Soames (*beat*) I see.
Irene You can imagine how embarrassed I felt when I had to reveal that I didn't have the faintest idea what she was talking about.
Soames I told Bosinney to tell no-one.
Irene Not even his future wife? Yes, that sounds like you. Well, I'm pleased to see Philip intends to share his life with June and not treat her the way you treat me—like a piece of property.
Soames (*lightly*) Oh, not that again, please. I'm sorry if I've caused you embarrassment. I thought you'd be pleased. And I'm presenting Bosinney with a splendid opportunity. It'll be the making of him.

Pause. Irene turns away

You don't want to go.
Irene Have my wishes anything to do with it?
Soames I was going to tell you when my mind was made up.
Irene Exactly! When *your* mind was made up! That was several weeks ago apparently, immediately after June's engagement party.
Soames Think, Irene. A house in the country. I honestly thought you'd like the very notion of that. I thought it would make you happy.

Irene How do you know what I like, what makes me happy?
Soames You never seem content here.
Irene And you thought because I'm not happy here I'd be happier locked away in some house in the middle of nowhere ...
Soames Locked away? As always, Irene, you're forever dramatizing.
Irene Don't you see, Soames? It's not a question of where I live. You can move me from place to place like a piece of furniture or one of your treasured paintings for all I care, but in truth I loathe you, Soames. I loathe the very sight of you!

Irene sweeps from the room

Soames sits down and sighs heavily

A Servant enters

Soames What is it?
Servant Mr Bosinney, sir.
Soames What, here?
Servant Yes, sir.

Soames sighs

Soames (*to himself*) I must say he has a wonderful sense of timing. (*To the Servant*) Show him in.

The Servant exits

Soames gets up and moves downstage

Bosinney enters

He immediately moves to a table and starts to unfold several drawings he has brought with him

Bosinney Mr Forsyte, sir. I'm sorry to come without an appointment, but I simply had to show you some of my initial sketches. They're not detailed, of course, merely impressions, but I have to confess I have been carried away. No! Inspired! That's the word. Absolutely inspired by the whole enterprise.
Soames I've found, Mr Bosinney, that inspiration usually costs a great deal of money.
Bosinney (*indicating to Soames to approach the sketches*) Come, sir. don't you want to see what your new home is going to look like?

Soames moves to the table and begins to look. There is a deafening silence. Bosinney walks about impatiently and arrogantly. Soames looks at him

(*Catching Soames's look, stopping pacing*) Well, sir?
Soames It's ... er ... it's an odd sort of house.

Bosinney stares at him for a moment

Bosinney Odd?
Soames Well ... yes ...

Bosinney moves to Soames's side and looks down at the sketches

Bosinney In what way—odd?

Soames Well ... it seems to me there's a lot of room cut to waste.

Bosinney (*moving away and walking about*) The principle of this house was that you should have room to breathe—like a gentleman.

Soames (*looking back at the papers and measuring a section between finger and thumb*) Oh, yes. I see.

Bosinney I've tried to plan a house with some vision. If you don't like it you'd better say so. After all who wants a house with vision when you can squeeze in an extra lavatory! I wish to point out that this elongated room has been especially designed to accommodate your pictures, divided from the inner covered courtyard by curtains. Draw them back and you'll have a space fifty-one by twenty-three, six. This double-faced stove in the centre, here, looks one way towards the inner courtyard, one way towards the picture room; this end wall is all window; you've a south-east light from that end and a north light from the courtyard end. You see, sir, in architecture as in life you cannot have vision without space. Some of the other architects sneer and call it modern. But it seems to me that it never occurs to these—older architects *so called*!—to embody the main principles of life in our buildings. They load our houses down with decoration gimcracks, corners, anything to distract the eye ...

Soames Excuse me, Bosinney but won't it look like a barrack!

Long pause. Bosinney stiffens and looks Soames straight in the eye

Bosinney I can see what it is. You want one of those mass-produced houses built by Mr Littlemaster, where the servants live in little pokey garrets and where all the houses look the same. By all means try one of those if you wish.

Bosinney moves away as if he's washed his hands of it. Soames continues to look at the drawings

Soames (*sighing*) Well ... it's—it's certainly original.

Bosinney (*turning triumphantly*) *Exactly!*

Soames (*smiling*) And—and it's a big place, too.

Bosinney (*returning to Soames*) Space, light, air. A modern way for a modern gentleman to live today.

Soames What about Mrs Forsyte? She can't stand the cold.

Bosinney I've thought of that. Look!

Soames looks at where Bosinney is pointing

I've given you hot water pipes in aluminium casings. You can get them with very good designs.

Soames continues looking

Soames Well, it's all very well, all this, but what is it going to cost?

Bosinney Hang the cost, sir!

Soames I beg your pardon?

Bosinney You've been to the site. You've seen the position, the magnificent views. It'll be the finest house outside London.

Soames And the most expensive, I shouldn't wonder.

Bosinney An investment, sir. Even without building on the site the land will treble its value in ten years. If you leave everything to me, the decorations, the landscaping of the gardens, everything, for a mere eight thousand five hundred pounds, I can build you a palace.

Soames looks at the sketches again

Soames A palace you say?

Irene enters carrying a tray. She is illuminated by Bosinney's presence

Irene Good-afternoon, Philip.

Bosinney (*visibly brightening*) Irene. (*He hurries to her*) Allow me.

He takes the tray from her and places it on a sidetable. Irene sits. Bosinney sits beside her

Irene Thank you.

Soames (*edged with sarcasm*) It seems the servants have abandoned us, Bosinney.

Irene (*ignoring the remark*) Tea, Philip?

Bosinney Thank you.

Irene pours while Soames continues to gaze at the sketches, his back to Bosinney and Irene

Soames Mr Bosinney has come to show us some sketches of our new house at Robin Hill, dear.

Irene (*unenthusiastically, yet looking admiringly at Bosinney and touching the lapel of his jacket fondly*) How exciting. Milk, Philip?

Bosinney Please.

Soames You wouldn't understand them of course.

Bosinney quickly kisses her hand

Irene In that case there's no point in showing them to me, is there?

Soames They're impressive, Bosinney.

Bosinney Thank you.

Soames turns abruptly and sees the look on Irene's face. She looks at Soames challengingly

Soames (*defiantly*) Go ahead, young man! Build me your palace!

The Lights fade

Bosinney and Irene exit. The Servant clears the tea tray

Soames moves DR

Scene 3

The same. Several months later, 1887

The Lights fade up on James and Soames

Soames Father, for the past ten minutes you've been doing everything but come to the point. Why *have* you come here this afternoon?
James To talk to you about the rumours ...
Soames What rumours?
James You mean to say you aren't aware of them? Your aunts have heard them.
Soames They hear what they want to hear ...
James There's no smoke without fire!
Soames ... so they can go around this family gossiping about what they *think* is happening and thereby pretend to be the fount of all knowledge!
James They are concerned about what is happening to you—as I am. Damn it, Soames, I'm your father!
Soames What is it that's happening to me?
James I've been to Robin Hill.
Soames You've been to Robin Hill.
James To see for myself. As no-one tells me anything anymore——

Soames sighs heavily at this

I decided to seek out Bosinney personally and ask him man to man.
Soames You may be my father but I resent the way you and those aunts of mine are interfering in my affairs.
James Resent? What's got into you, Soames? What self-respecting father would refrain from doing anything when he sees his only son being ridiculed by all and sundry?
Soames (*dismissively*) All and sundry! Who is this all and sundry?
James This family has a position to live up to and to protect. Because of this I went and spoke to Bosinney. I said it before and I say it again, I don't like the fellow. Much too arrogant for my liking. And he's spending your money like water.
Soames I know what he's spending.
James If you know then you're a bigger fool than I take you for.

Soames is about to protest but James carries on

I know I may seem a little hard on you, but can't you see what this young man is doing?
Soames He's building me a house, Father. A fine house. He says it'll be a palace.
James A palace be damned! It's a white elephant. What self-respecting Forsyte and businessman builds a house outside London? No Forsyte has ever considered moving to the country. My God, there's nothing there!

Soames I intend to break with tradition.
James Why? For what purpose?
Soames That is my business
James Is it what Irene wants?

No reply

Is it?
Soames That is between Irene and myself.
James (*shaking with anger*) Irene!
Soames Why do you say it like that?
James It's about time you had some children, Soames. Irene has too much time on her hands.
Somes Please, Father ...
James All right, maybe that has nothing to do with me, but the way you're throwing money at this new house of yours, is! I'll not have the City laughing at your financial ineptitude!
Soames Ineptitude?
James Yes. What else would you call it? You're allowing this man to spend your money at will. When I asked him if he knew how much he'd spent over and above the agreed sum of eight thousand five hundred pounds he wouldn't tell me. He looked me straight in the eye and said he didn't know. After all these months and he doesn't *know* how much he's spent. And why should he when all he has to do is come round here and ask for another blank cheque!
Soames Stop it, Father! *Stop it!*

Irene enters

James That man's a charlatan!

Both men see Irene and become silent

Irene I could hear you upstairs. *And* so could the servants!
Soames Excuse me!

Soames hurries from the room

There is a long pause. James sits down breathless

James I apologize for my behaviour, Irene. Shouting like a common tradesman. Most unbecoming.
Irene It's the first time I've heard you and Soames quarrel.
James And I sincerely hope it will be the last.
Irene If it's about the house ...
James The matter is between Soames and myself.
Irene Yes, of course. The topic of our new house is not a subject on which I can be permitted to comment, is it?

They look directly at one another

James Why don't you have a child?

The directness of the question startles Irene

Irene (*catching her breath*) What?
James You heard me, madam. Why don't you have a child?
Irene Because we don't choose to.
James We? Don't you mean *you*?
Irene I don't think this concerns you. (*She turns to go*)
James Soames is desperate for a son and I'd like to have another grandson before I die. Think about it, Irene, before you bring ruin on Soames and yourself.
Irene I don't know what you mean.
James I'm not blind. I can see the sadness in my son's eyes. And I can see the hatred in yours. But, I wonder, what look is in those eyes when you make all those secret trips to Robin Hill?
Irene What are you talking about?
James I was told certain things. For someone, whom I believe doesn't want to live in her new home, the visits you make to the site seem puzzling to say the least. I'm head of this family, Irene. I will not preside over its ruin by scandal caused by you or anyone else.
Irene I'm very much obliged to you.
James Whatever is going on between you and ... a certain young man, I want it to stop. You're a married woman. Carry out your wifely duties. Have a child. And behave like a true Forsyte!

James exits

The Lights fade to half as Irene moves downstage and sits, shaken by James's outburst

Scene 4

The same. A week later

The Lights come up to full

Soames enters

Irene I didn't hear you come in.
Soames (*moving to her side*) I thought you might have been in the park on such a beautiful day.
Irene It's too hot.
Soames I see. (*He sits down*)
Irene (*getting up*) I'll arrange for some tea.
Soames (*placing his hand on her arm*) Sit down.

She stops

Please.

Irene sits

Have you ... er ... been sitting here ... waiting ... expecting someone?
Irene Yes. That is—not particularly.
Soames Whom may I ask?

Irene (*breathing nervously; after a pause*) Mr Bosinney said he might call.

Soames He ought to be at work.

Irene doesn't reply. Soames gets up

I'd like you to come to the stores with me. After that we can go to the park.

Irene I don't want to go out. I have a headache.

Soames If ever I want to do anything you always have headache. It'll do you good to sit outside. We can find a tree to sit under ...

Irene doesn't respond. Long pause

I don't know what your idea of a wife's duty is. I have never known.

Still no reply

I have tried to do what you want. It's not my fault that I haven't been able to put my heart into it.

Irene You're forgetting something.

Soames Oh?

Irene The promise you made before we married.

Soames Promise? What promise?

Irene It was more than a promise. You made an oath, Soames.

Soames I don't know what you're talking about. I know of no oath.

Irene I remember the day well. It was warm like today, three years ago, and you were seated on the fallen trunk of a tree. Already you had asked me to marry you on four occasions and already you had promised, oh, at least twenty times, that if our marriage were not a success then I should be free as if we had never married. On this occasion I asked you to swear it. And you did.

Soames No!

Irene You did, Soames. You swore to let me go!

Soames I don't remember!

Irene Are you saying you lied then as you're lying now?

Soames How dare you accuse me of that when all the time you ... (*He stops*)

Irene I'm asking you again, Soames. (*Beat*) I'm begging you. Let me go.

Soames turns away, secretly alarmed

Soames Let you go? You don't know what you're talking about. Let you go? How can I let you go? We're married. For God's sake don't let's hear any more of such nonsense. Put your hat on and come and sit in the park with me.

Irene Then you won't let me go?

Soames What on earth would you do with yourself if I did? You have no money.

Irene I could manage somehow.

Soames (*moving to Irene with mounting anger*) Understand once and for all. I won't have you talking like this. Go and put your hat on.

She remains silent

(*Angrily*) I suppose you don't want to miss Bosinney if he comes!

Irene gets up and exits

Soames hurries to exit, intending to pursue the argument but he thinks better of it and returns downstage to calm himself

Damn! (*He sits down*)

After a moment, Irene enters carrying her hat

Soames stands, thinking he has triumphed. He moves towards her

I see you've come to your senses. (*He goes to take her arm*)
Irene Don't touch me!

Soames recoils from her sudden hatred and tries to regain his dignity. Pause

Soames (*a hardness entering his voice*) You will no doubt be interested to know that I've been discussing with my father what we should do about Bosinney.
Irene What do you mean?
Soames He has exceeded his instructions regarding Robin Hill yet again. He's gone over the final figure by a further four hundred pounds without any adequate explanation.
Irene Oh, four hundred pounds . . .
Soames (*with rising anger*) A small figure to you no doubt . . .
Irene I dare say you can afford it.
Soames I don't intend paying it.
Irene What do you mean?
Soames (*a growing uneasiness*) You'll know soon enough. A mere trifle, quite beneath your contempt, four hundred pounds . . .
Irene Do you mean that you're going to make *him* pay the sum towards that hateful house?
Soames Yes! I do.
Irene You know he has nothing?
Soames Yes!
Irene Then you are meaner than I thought.

He moves threateningly towards her

Soames Good! Tell me, madam! Are you having an affair with Bosinney?
Irene No! I am not!

They look at one another. Soames stands back not knowing whether to believe her or not

Soames I believe you are made of stone.
Irene Not I. It is you who is made of stone.

Soames suddenly and viciously grabs her arm. She is shaken by this action and cries out

Soames A good beating is the only thing that will bring you to your senses.

They look at one another with mutual hatred

Soames releases her arm and storms out

The Lights fade to a Black-out. Irene remains, looking after Soames

Young Jo, fair haired and aged about thirty-nine, enters with a book and sits L *and begins to read*

Irene moves to C *and starts to pace up and down as the Lights fade up to full*

Scene 5

The Botanical Gardens. The following day

Bosinney enters and moves towards C

Bosinney (*approaching*) Irene ...

Irene (*going to him*) Oh, Philip, thank heavens you could come. (*She embraces and kisses him*)

Bosinney You said it was urgent.

Irene Events are beginning to overtake us.

Bosinney What do you mean?

Irene I believe Soames knows. His father certainly does.

Bosinney What's happened then? Soames hasn't hurt you, has he?

Irene No ... but sometimes ... he frightens me.

Bosinney We must go somewhere ...

Irene Where?

Bosinney Abroad. We could go abroad. Cut ourselves free ...

Irene With nothing to live on? You haven't any money. Nor, as Soames keeps reminding me, have I.

Bosinney We'd manage somehow. Oh, Irene, think of it. Just ourselves to consider. No social obligations, no conventions to observe and above all no Forsytes! Just the freedom you've always wanted.

Irene How can we be free? No, my darling. I love you for the thought but what you suggest is impossible and in your heart you know it.

Bosinney Then how long must we endure hiding in corners and meeting like this?

Irene Until Soames agrees to a divorce. We have no alternative. And he will in time. In the months ahead you can establish yourself and become the best architect in London. (*She smiles at him*) I have every confidence in you.

Bosinney But I want to be with you now, not tomorrow, not next month.

Irene I know, but you must be patient. In the meantime we had better be careful. I can't come and see you at Robin Hill anymore.

Bosinney Why should the Forsytes be allowed to make me feel like a criminal?

Irene Because in their eyes that is exactly what you are. You are trying to take away something that belongs to them. (*She brings his hand up to stroke her cheek. Whispering*) I love you.

Bosinney Perhaps if I spoke to Soames.

Irene No! No, you mustn't do that. That would ruin everything, including your career. Please do as I say and be patient. Soames is suffering just as much as we are. Let's not forget that. All I ask of you now is to be careful. (*She kisses his cheek*) I'll leave first. I'll be in touch, my darling. Goodbye.

Irene exits upstage

Bosinney looks after her and then sits C. *After a moment, Jo gets up and moves to Bosinney*

Jo Excuse me.

Bosinney Yes?

Jo I'm Jolyon Forsyte.

Bosinney Forsyte? We haven't met, have we?

Jo No. I'm the black sheep of the family. I'm June's father.

Bosinney (*after a pause; greatly embarrassed*) Oh . . . (*He goes to rise*)

Jo Please! Don't get up. (*He sits*)

Bosinney Have you been following me?

Jo Yes.

Bosinney Why?

Jo I have to speak to you. I had no knowledge we would end up here.

Bosinney You followed me all the way from the Club?

Jo You did leave in rather a hurry.

Bosinney I didn't know you were a member.

Jo (*smiling*) We Forsytes are everywhere.

Bosinney So it would seem.

Jo Excuse me for asking but was that Irene Forsyte just now?

Bosinney Don't you know your own cousin?

Jo My dear Bosinney, I was condemned to the wilderness when I left my wife for June's governess long before Soames and Irene married. Like you I also played with fire.

Bosinney And no doubt the family took delight in burning your fingers, too?

Jo The family always tries to destroy what it doesn't understand. Still, time's a great healer. After fourteen years my father came to see me and informed me of June's engagement to you.

Bosinney That was very solicitous of him.

Jo I believe it was more in June's interests than mine since in doing so he also took the opportunity of telling me how distraught she was by the rumours concerning you and her dearest friend, confirmed I might add, by what I've just witnessed. So my father, in his wisdom, thought it best to take her away for a while and see whether his prodigal son could help in any way—presumably, I imagine, because I have experience of such—delicate matters.

Bosinney I must say I find it difficult to think of you as a Forsyte.

Jo However, I think it wise, in the circumstances, that you do.

Bosinney Are you here to threaten me, sir?

Jo Mr Bosinney, in a short time you seem to have had a profound effect on several members of our family. Soames, I gather, has been in acrimonious correspondence with you over the mounting costs of the house ...

Bosinney You have been well briefed.

Jo You find all this humorous, do you? Remember, June is my daughter ...

Bosinney A daughter, sir, you readily abandoned.

Jo I advise you not to interfere in matters you know very little about. I'm here merely to——

Bosinney Warn me?

Jo You do have the habit of "jumping in", Mr Bosinney, don't you? I'm here to ... "point out", that whether we like it or not it doesn't do to despise a Forsyte or disregard them.

Bosinney But didn't you do precisely that yourself?

Jo I don't recommend that every man should follow my path. No. All I will say is to break up a home is at best dangerous and selfish into the bargain. (*Standing*) Mr Bosinney, you are in danger and it amazes me that you don't see it. Soames will destroy you. He has the reason. And, above all, he has the means.

Bosinney Ah, so it was for *my* benefit that you are here?

Jo I came here to try and reason with a man. Instead I seem to have found a fool! Good-day, sir.

Jo leaves

Bosinney looks after him. The Lights fade to half

Bosinney leaves. The Aunts and James enter and sit R, *while a Servant places a tray of tea on the table. He hands the cups round during the following. The Lights come up*

Scene 6

Soames's house in Knightsbridge. Several days later

Aunt Juley June's back at last.

James Is she?

Aunt Juley So I hear.

James Well, that's more than I hear, Juley. But then no-one tells me anything.

Aunt Hester She returned with Old Jolyon yesterday morning. From Switzerland.

James Switzerland! Damn foreign place! Why he couldn't have taken her to Broadstairs, God only knows. Good air, Broadstairs.

Aunt Juley I wonder how much she actually knows.

James About what?

Aunt Juley Oh, for heaven's sake, James. What do you think? About Bosinney and Irene and what's been going on while she's been up a mountain or whatever tourists do in Switzerland.

Aunt Hester Juley! Irene may hear you.

Aunt Juley Don't be silly, Hester. She's out. She won't have the courage to face us. And where's Soames by the way?

Aunt Hester He's talking to someone in the study. He'll be down shortly.

Aunt Juley It's just that he *did* invite us and here we are being *kept waiting like trades-people*!

Aunt Hester (*smiles*) Do you think we're going to be ticked off?

Aunt Juley Ticked off? No-one ticks me off! Anyway, what have *we* done to be ticked off by Soames of all people?

Aunt Hester (*heavily*) Well . . .

Aunt Juley You say that, Hester, as if I should feel guilty about something or other.

James We *know* the ones who should feel guilty.

Aunt Juley Exactly, James. I don't see why *I* should feel guilty.

Aunt Hester I never said you should, dear. It's just that we have been playing an active part——

Aunt Juley —in getting at the truth, Hester. That's all. That's the only reason we went with James to Robin Hill that day. To get at the truth.

Aunt Hester (*peering ahead to see where her cup is*) I can't see how Soames has been so blind.

Aunt Juley (*picking up the cup and handing it to her*) Neither can I, dear. Neither can I. But there you are, men are fools when it comes to matters of the heart. Not that I've had that trouble myself. Septimus, bless him, was as weak as dishwater. He was Small by name and small by nature.

Aunt Hester I can thank my lucky stars I didn't marry, then.

Aunt Juley I dread to think what you'd have brought home, Hester, with eyesight like yours.

Aunt Hester I wish you wouldn't keep on about my eyes, Juley. They're failing because I'm old. Remember you're old, too, something of *yours* might fail before long.

Aunt Juley If I'm going to fail I'm going the Forsyte way. I shall fail altogether not in bits and pieces.

James This conversation is becoming depressing.

Aunt Juley Not nearly as depressing as the scandal that threatens to engulf this family, James. It's about time something was done about it.

Aunt Hester Maybe that's why Soames has called us here today.

Aunt Juley Let us hope so. We *should* be the first to know of any developments. After all we're virtually the oldest members of the family except for Old Jolyon of course. And he's so old everyone *thinks* he's dead anyway.

James Jolyon surprised me the other day when I met him at the Club.

Aunt Juley Oh? In what way?

James I really can't say anything. Professional etiquette, you know.

Aunt Juley We're family, James. We don't have secrets!

Aunt Hester In the present circumstances, Juley, that sounds somewhat hollow.

Aunt Juley You know what I mean, Hester. Come on, James. (*Boldly*) You *know* it won't go any further.

James (*giving the Aunts a very old-fashioned look*) I can't go into details, you understand, but Old Jolyon is changing his will.

Aunt Juley } (*together*) { No. In what way?
Aunt Hester } { No.

James He's asked me to draw up papers whereby Jo gets an annuity and June will have the rest immediately upon his death.

Aunt Juley But that could be in excess of—of—one hundred thousand a year.

James I shouldn't be at all surprised.

Aunt Juley Well, her trip to Switzerland certainly proved fruitful didn't it?

Aunt Hester Juley! (*She peers ahead looking for the table on which to place her cup*)

Aunt Juley Straight ahead, dear.

Aunt Hester Thank you.

Aunt Juley So June's settled for life, then?

Aunt Hester And so is Jo. I'm sure that's right.

Aunt Juley That's typical of you, Hester. All the scandal he brought down upon this family and now he receives an annuity for his pains.

Soames enters

James Ah, my boy.

Soames I'm sorry I kept you all waiting. I see you've had some tea ...

Aunt Juley Get to the point, Soames. Why did you summon us here?

Soames As blunt as ever, Aunt.

Aunt Hester She doesn't mean it, Soames. How are you?

Soames Well, thank you.

Aunt Hester And Irene?

A sudden silence. James coughs

Soames (*riding it*) As well as can be expected. Now, I asked you to come here because I thought you ought to know what action I propose to take.

Aunt Juley Yes?

Soames Concerning Mr Bosinney.

James Ah, good.

Soames Apparently he has been ignoring my instructions about his extravagance on the house at Robin Hill. We agreed on a final sum of twelve thousand pounds, including the overspending to date ...

James Twelve thousand pounds? I never thought it had gone that far.

Soames Well, Father, I'm afraid it has. I partially blame myself, of course, but this upstart has no honour. And he's a liar into the bargain. *And* in spite of a warning, given to him only a few weeks ago, he has spent a further four hundred pounds over some decoration or other without even consulting me. I therefore intend to make him pay for it—to the hilt!

James Then you're taking him to court?

Soames Yes. I have instigated proceedings. I have just been finalizing details with my clerk.

James Splendid, my boy. Splendid.

Soames I've decided to crush him, Father. To send him into oblivion ...

James That'll teach him to flout the wishes of our family . . .
Soames . . . I've had enough. Soon, Mr Bosinney will be no more!
Aunt Juley And . . . er . . . is that all you wish to tell us?
Soames Why yes. I can't think of anything else. (*He smiles*) So, my dear aunts, you can spread that piece of gossip around the family circle at your pleasure. Soames is acting at last!

The Lights fade to half. Piano music

The Aunts and James exit. A Servant clears the cups and tray

Soames moves DR *and sits.*

SCENE 7

The same. A few weeks later

The ripple of firelight from an imaginary fire downstage begins to illuminate Soames's brooding face. The sound of a barrel organ is heard outside

Irene enters upstage and takes off her cloak while gazing at her happy image in an imaginary mirror

Soames slowly rises

Soames Very pretty!

Irene shudders as she spins around. She makes to leave

Why such a hurry?
Irene Let me go. (*She put her hand up and smooths back a curl*)
Soames I don't like that blouse. It's a soft, shapeless thing!

Soames grabs the blouse. Irene tries to get away. The blouse rips

Irene Don't touch me!
Soames And where have you been?
Irene (*beat*) In heaven—out of this house.

Irene moves away again and Soames follows her

Soames Why *him*? Eh? Why Bosinney? Why not me?

He roughly turns her around to face him. She becomes more fearful

Look at me! You think he loves you? He doesn't love you.
Irene And you do, I suppose?
Soames You know I do.
Irene To possess! Not to love! It's late. I'm tired.
Soames Bosinney tired you out, has he? Not for him the excuse of a headache. Tell me, Irene. What do I have to do, eh? What do I have to do to measure up to this—this architect?

Irene tries to leave again

Stay where you are! (*Low*) Madam! Last night you locked your door against me. Me! Your husband! You sent me back to my room like something—unwanted. Yet, don't you understand, *can't* you understand that you are the only one to appease my hunger, my love for you. (*Then, a sudden agonizing pleading*) Irene ... please ... I want a son. Give me a son, Irene. You must!

Irene (*drawing away horrified*) You have to let me go!

Again Irene tries to leave but Soames grabs her

Take your hands off me!

Soames You are mine! Forever!

Irene I'm not! I'm not your anything!

Soames If you can't be mine you're certainly not going to be *his*!

Irene No, Soames ... don't.

Soames (*his anger now turning into fury*) I'm your husband, Irene, and my God I have rights ...

Irene (*looking at him in horror*) *No!*

Soames I have rights, Irene. *I have rights!*

He forces her down on to the settee and falls on top of her as she struggles violently. The sound of the barrel organ rises to a crescendo as the Lights quickly fade to a Black-out. The barrel organ stops suddenly. Silence

Soames and Irene exit in the darkness

Scene 8

The same. Several weeks later

The Lights come up to full

James and Soames enter wearing top coats having just returned from the law courts

James Well, Soames my boy. You won! Bosinney is ruined.

Soames (*solemnly*) Yes, he is.

James He'll be declared bankrupt I shouldn't wonder. Mind you, it doesn't seem to have caused him concern. The man didn't even turn up to defend himself. (*He smiles*) Yes, most satisfactory. (*Then, seeing Soames's glum face*) You're not ill, are you, Soames?

Soames No, Father.

James In that case let's go to the Club and celebrate. Come along.

Soames Strange, wouldn't you say ...?

James What?

Soames Bosinney not being in court.

James The man's a coward.

Soames He didn't strike me the sort to give in.

James Come along, Soames. I know it's not very pleasant to wash one's dirty linen in public, but what's done is done. Let's go to the Club and forget all this business ...

Soames If you don't mind, Father, I don't feel like celebrating.

James What's the matter with you? You won! Doesn't that mean anything to you?

Soames A measly four hundred pounds?

James It isn't the money we all know that. What's important is that you ruined the young upstart. You did what you set out to do. You crushed him!

Soames Somehow I don't think I have. I know what you're hoping for, Father, but I don't think it's made any difference. (*Beat*) Irene has left me.

Pause

James Left you?

Soames So, I ask myself, who has won and who has lost?

James Left you? You never told me she was going to leave.

Soames How could I tell?

James I don't know what to say, Soames.

Soames That's a pity, Father, because I was going to ask you; what's to be done?

James (*tetchily*) How do I know what's to be done? What's the good of asking me? Nobody tells me anything anymore and they still come and ask me what's to be done.

Pause

(*Then kindly*) You must go after her, I suppose.

Soames But I don't know where she's gone.

James Don't know where she's gone? How do you mean, you don't know where she's gone? Where do you suppose she's gone? She's gone after that young Bosinney, hasn't she? You said so yourself.

Soames sighs heavily. A sad figure, he looks beaten

James There'll be a scandal. I always said there would. (*He sighs*) Well, I can't help you, Soames. I'm getting too old. (*He moves slowly to the exit*) Go and get her back, my boy. That's what you'll have to do. (*He turns*) Soames? Did you hear me?

Soames Sorry, Father I was thinking. The only decent thing she did was to leave her jewel case behind.

James looks at him and then exits

Soames is left alone as the Lights fade to a black-out

Soames exits in the darkness

Scene 9

Bosinney's rooms. Later the same day

The Lights come up C *on June sitting in a chair deep in thought. Her only sign of anxiety is the continual twisting of a handkerchief in her hands*

Suddenly, we hear a door bang, off

June (*getting up*) Phil? Phil? Is that you?

Irene enters carrying a small bunch of violets

June is surprised and angry, to say the least, at Irene's presence. They stand, just looking at one another

(*After a pause*) What have you come for?

Irene doesn't reply, but turns away

(*Almost an excuse for her presence*) This terrible case. I came to tell him . . .

Irene turns to face June who breaks down

He lost, Irene. He lost! (*Getting no response from Irene, angrily*) Don't stand there as if you were made of stone!

Irene (*laughing a little*) I wish to God I were!

June (*turning away*) Don't say a word. I don't want to hear what you've come for . . .

Irene (*almost pleadingly*) Where is he, June?

June (*angry but helpless*) Stop! I don't want to hear! All I know is we can't both stay in this room together!

A smile crosses Irene's face

You have no right here, Irene!

Irene I have no right anywhere.

June (*after a beat*) What do you mean?

Irene I have left Soames. I think you always wanted me to.

June (*putting her hands to her ears*) I don't want to *hear* anything. I don't want to *know* anything. It's impossible to fight you. Why don't you go?

Irene Where would I go?

June looks at her and is about to reply but the way Irene nervously twists the bunch of violets in her hand makes her pull back. There is a silence between them for a moment and then we become aware that June is now quietly sobbing

June (*through her tears*) How could you come? You have been a false friend to me.

Irene laughs a little. June turns and becomes angry again

Why have you come? You've ruined my life! And now you want to ruin his!

Suddenly Irene raises the violets to cover her quivering mouth. June moves forward a little in a conciliatory gesture

Please, Irene.

Irene hurries from the room with June following her

(*Calling as she goes*) Irene! Irene!

The door bangs, off

After a brief moment, June returns and sits in the chair sobbing

The Lights fade to a Black-out

Scene 10

Soames's house in Knightsbridge. An hour later

The Lights come up on Irene, dressed as before, huddled in a chair

Soames enters

Soames So you've come back?

Irene attempts to rise. He prevents her

No! Stay there.

Irene sits again

Why is all this? Why should I suffer so? What have I done? It is not my fault? Why do you think you can walk out of this house to be with your lover and then, when it doesn't work out to your satisfaction, return here with equanimity? Do you take me for a fool?

Irene What do you want me to say? Do you want me to beg? Here? Now? All right. I beg, Soames. I beg to be left alone. To stay. Is that the satisfaction you require?

A figure appears in the shadows upstage. It is young Jo

Soames turns

Soames (*sharply*) What is it you want, sir?

Irene leaps to her feet thinking the visitor is Bosinney. She turns away in despair on seeing it is a stranger

Jo Forgive me, sir. The door was open. Might I see your wife for a moment. I have a message for her.

Soames Good Lord! Young Jo Forsyte! Can it really be a co-incidence that you and my wife are here in the same room together? Both having brought dishonour to the family name?

Jo It is no co-incidence, sir. The purpose of my visit concerns one Philip Bosinney.

Irene turns to face him

He was killed this afternoon. A street accident. He . . . he may have taken his own life.

Irene gives a distressed gasp at this

I think it better for the family as a whole if we, in common with the police, come to the conclusion that it was an accident.

Soames (*after a pause*) Yes. You may well be right.
Jo I'm sure I am. It is with this in mind, sir, that I have come to speak with Irene.
Soames As it's about Bosinney you will appreciate that I have no wish to be present. As far as I am concerned the man did the only decent thing he could in the circumstances. I for one have no regrets about his death.

Soames exits

Long pause. Jo moves to Irene

Jo I will be brief, but rest assured, dear cousin, that I am your friend and wish you no harm.
Irene Thank you.
Jo I know how you must feel.
Irene No, cousin, you don't. (*Beat. She turns away*) Even the *thought* of returning here, to be under the same roof with ...
Jo I am not here to apportion blame. I'm sure Soames loves you in his way as you love him in yours—in spite of everything.
Irene Love him? I hate him! You have no idea how much I hate Soames but I have nowhere else to go.
Jo (*holding out his hand*) I've come to return this to you.
Irene What is it?
Jo It was found on Bosinney's body.

Irene takes the handkerchief

It is yours I believe. The initials are the same.
Irene (*taking it almost reverently*) Yes, it is mine.
Jo My father was anxious it should not fall into the wrong hands.
Irene Thank you. You've been a good friend.
Jo (*taking her hands in his*) Good-night, cousin.
Irene Good-night, Jo.
Jo I hope we shall meet again. Good-night.

The Lights fade to half

Young Jo and Irene take their leave. A Servant enters with a tray of cakes and sandwiches and the Aunts enter and sit down to have tea

The Lights come up to full

Scene 11

The same. Twelve years later, 1899

The Aunts are wearing mourning. Aunt Juley sighs deeply as she sits

Aunt Juley Well, that's another Forsyte gone. So! Who's left? (*She looks around the room*)
Aunt Hester Roger *was* eighty-six, dear.

Aunt Juley It wasn't old age that killed him, Hester. He'd be alive today if he hadn't preferred German mutton to all the other brands.

Aunt Hester (*having discovered the sandwiches*) He always did possess a somewhat eccentric digestion.

Aunt Juley So will you if you pick like that, dear.

Aunt Hester Funerals make me hungry.

Aunt Juley You haven't had to attend that many, Hester. Not until recently anyway. (*She sighs*) Unfortunately, we Forsytes seem to be dropping like flies.

Aunt Hester Dropping we may be, dear, but we do seem to live to a good old age. Old Jolyon was in his eighties when he passed away seven years ago.

Aunt Juley True. And James is still going strong—just!

Aunt Hester Where is James?

Aunt Juley Trying to get out of the carriage. The last few years have not been kind to him, I'm afraid. Apart from not remembering anything he's now as deaf as a post so he can't hear what he can't remember hearing in the first place!

Aunt Hester (*smiling*) Poor James. As we came in Soames was trying to get him up the steps and into the house.

Aunt Juley You make our brother sound like a trunk!

Aunt Hester Now *there's* someone who's aged.

Aunt Juley Who?

Aunt Hester Soames.

Aunt Juley Really? I thought the years had been kind to him—considering. In fact, I thought he looked younger. Especially since he's fallen in love again.

Aunt Hester Juley be careful! He might hear you.

Aunt Juley So what? Everyone knows.

Aunt Hester You do surprise me. I thought Soames had been more discreet.

Aunt Juley Well, James knows and if the news has reached him you can be sure the rest of London knew about it ages ago.

Aunt Hester The whole affair's most unfortunate. I don't know where it will end. After all, he can't do anything until he divorces Irene. As far as I can gather James isn't at all happy with this new liaison.

Aunt Juley That's because she's French! You know James. He trusts nothing that is foreign.

Aunt Hester And with good cause when you consider what's happening out in South Africa at the moment.

Aunt Juley That's the Dutch for you. They've always been peculiar. (*Looking around*) Where are they?

Aunt Hester Holland. Where do you expect them to be?

Aunt Juley No, no! James and Soames. They must be in the house by now.

Aunt Hester They're probably discussing business, dear. Like all true Forsytes they won't let a funeral stand in the way of making money.

Aunt Juley That's why we're a great family, Hester.

Aunt Hester Oh, I wasn't criticizing, dear. Simply making an observation.

Still, with Roger gone the senior Forsytes are becoming somewhat thin on the ground, wouldn't you say?

Aunt Juley There are plenty of young ones sprouting up to take our place, Hester.

Aunt Hester I don't know whether "sprouting up" is an apt phrase, Juley, but I know what you mean. I just wish the family were more united that's all. After all, Old Jolyon made peace with Jo after fourteen years of silence. I don't see why Soames cannot take the broader view too and do the same.

Aunt Juley That's rather a lot to ask, isn't it? That side of the family has interfered in Soames's affairs—even to the extent of Old Jolyon buying Robin Hill.

Aunt Hester I can quite understand Soames's reluctance in living there himself after what happened with Bosinney and Irene and all that ...

Aunt Juley And when you come to think of it, our dear brother didn't help there either, did he?

Aunt Hester That's true.

Aunt Juley When Soames was expecting Irene to crawl back full of remorse after leaving him for good, what does dear Old Jolyon go and do? Leaves her fifteen thousand pounds so making her independent for life! I mean if that wasn't pouring oil on troubled waters ... No, Irene played her cards rather carefully. She has a cup of tea with our brother, spins him a hard luck story and the old fool falls for it. How gullible can a man get?

Aunt Hester Be fair, Juley. I think it was rather more than just having a cup of tea. Jolyon and Irene became very close when she finally left Soames.

Aunt Juley Frankly, I don't know why Soames put up with it. He should have thrown her out of the house when she came home the night Bosinney killed himself. Not let the whole affair drag on for another twelve years. She's brought nothing but shame on this family and made Soames miserable into the bargain.

Aunt Hester She made Jolyon happy in the remaining months of his life.

Aunt Juley Huh! She was after his money. And she got it!

Aunt Hester And she uses it to help the less fortunate in our society, so I hear.

Aunt Juley Conscience!

Aunt Hester Not so. I hear it was out of gratitude to that down-and-out woman who prevented her from throwing herself in the Thames soon after Bosinney's death.

Aunt Juley Well, that good Samaritan, whoever she was, doesn't earn *my* gratitude.

Aunt Hester That's a wicked thing to say.

Aunt Juley You may be able to forgive her, Hester, for what she's done to this family, but I can't ...

James enters assisted by Soames. James is now quite crotchety

And I don't suppose Soames will either.

Soames What's that, Aunt Juley?

Aunt Juley Nothing, Soames.
Soames I heard my name mentioned if I'm not mistaken.
Aunt Hester Where have you been? The tea is cold.

Soames helps James to the chair

James Discussing business.
Aunt Juley (*to Hester*) There! I told you.
Soames While you, I suspect dear Aunt, were spreading more scandal as usual.
Aunt Juley Seems to run in the family, wouldn't you say, Soames? At least in two branches of it!
Soames As blunt as ever, Aunt.
James What's that?
Soames Nothing, Father. Just discussing Aunt Juley's tittle-tattle.
James Oh, that. There is too much tittle-tattle in this family if you ask me.
Aunt Juley What would you prefer, James? More tittle and less tattle?
James What?
Aunt Juley Nothing.
James No-one tells me anything anymore ...
Aunt Juley The last few years have seen great changes in this family. One can't ignore them. One can't pretend they never happened.
Soames But you, Aunt, seem to make more of them than they really deserve. You almost make a fetish of them.
Aunt Juley Fetish?
Aunt Hester Please don't quarrel! There's enough fighting in the world with those awful Boers rampaging all over South Africa.
James What's that about Boers?
Aunt Juley Oh, don't start him off on that, Hester ...
James I know what I'd do with them if I were in command out there.
Aunt Juley As no-one ever tells you anything, James, you'd never receive a command to act upon.
James That's right, Juley. Make fun of me. I can't help going deaf you know ...
Aunt Juley You hear what you want to hear when it suits you.
Aunt Hester Don't agitate him, Juley. It's bad for his heart.
James What's that?
Aunt Hester Nothing, James. Nothing.
James That's what you always say, Hester. Nothing. Yet your lips seem to move an awful lot. I'm not blind you know.
Aunt Juley I was just about to chastise Soames for not coming to Roger's funeral. After all that *was* the purpose of our visit.
James She's right, Soames. Why didn't you come, eh? The whole family was talking about it. No Forsyte has ever missed a funeral.
Aunt Juley (*aside*) I don't suppose any of us will!
James What's that?
Aunt Juley Never mind, James.
Soames I couldn't come because I am waiting for someone.
Aunt Hester Really? May we ask whom?

Soames Irene if you must know.

James I don't want to hear that woman's name mentioned in my presence!

Aunt Juley (*to Soames*) Irene?

James Didn't you hear?

Aunt Hester Did you say *Irene*?

James (*almost demented*) I said I didn't want her name mentioned in my presence and I meant it!

Soames Calm yourself, Father.

Aunt Juley I thought you had sworn never to have her in the house again.

Soames I did. But I needed to see her on a personal matter and as I am the injured party in the affair I decided to ask her to come and see me—with the help of Jo Forsyte.

Aunt Juley
Aunt Hester } (*together*) Jo Forsyte?

Everyone freezes

The Lights crossfade quickly to a spotlight C *on Young Jo and Irene*

Irene (*sitting*) Please, sit down.

Jo Thank you. (*He does so*) You look unchanged.

Irene And you look younger, Cousin Jolyon.

Jo (*running his hands through his hair*) I'm ancient but I don't feel it. That's one thing about painting. It keeps you young. Titian lived to ninety-nine and had to have the plague to kill him off. The first time I ever saw you I thought of a picture by him.

Irene When did you see me for the first time?

Jo In the Botanical Gardens.

Irene How did you know it was me, if you hadn't seen me before?

Jo By someone who came up to you.

Irene I see.

Jo I remember the look on your faces. I wondered at the time; was this a moment of joy or a moment of tragedy . . .?

Irene It was many lives ago.

Jo (*after a beat*) What *is* your recipe for youth, Irene?

Irene People who aren't allowed to live remain wonderfully preserved. Haven't you noticed? (*She smiles*)

Jo Which, by implication I imagine, brings us to Soames—the reason for my visit. He came to see me the day before yesterday—as your Trustee. He wants a divorce.

Irene Really?

Jo Do you?

Irene After all these years? It's rather late. Won't it be difficult?

Jo Not unless . . .

Irene I have a lover? I've never had a lover since Philip.

Jo (*taken aback by her frankness*) Still, I suppose you would give a great deal to be free, too?

Irene I don't know. What does it matter now?

Jo Supposing you were to love again?

Irene Then I should love.

Pause. They both look at one another. Jo breaks first

Jo Is there anything you would like me to say to him?
Irene Only I'm sorry he's not free. He had his chance once. I don't know why he didn't take it.
Jo Because he's a Forsyte. We never part with things, you know, unless we want something in their place and not always then.
Irene So ... what does Soames want in place of me?
Jo I don't know. Children, perhaps.

Pause

Irene It's hard for him, I see that. I would help him to be free if I could.

Jo looks at the floor in embarrassment

Jo (*standing*) Well, I shall have to see Soames. If there is anything I can do for you I'm always at your service. You must think I'm a wretched substitute for my father.
Irene Your dear, dear father. I owe him much.
Jo At all events, I'll let you know what happens when I speak to Soames. He may supply the necessary material himself.
Irene (*shaking her head*) Oh, no. You see he has too much to lose; and I have nothing. I should like him to be free—I really would—but I don't see what I can do.
Jo Nor I at the moment. (*He turns to go*)
Irene Cousin Jolyon? What's the lady's name?

Jo turns back

The reason for Soames sending you here? His new acquisition?
Jo Annette.
Irene Annette?
Jo She's French.
Irene Indeed. And does she know he's still married?

The Lights crossfade to R *as before*

Irene and Young Jo exit. A Servant enters R

Servant Mrs Forsyte is here, sir.

Silence suddenly descends

Aunt Juley I'm leaving!
Aunt Hester Please, Juley.
James What's happening?
Soames Show her in.
Aunt Juley Soames!
Soames You can't escape the inescapable, Aunt. She's right outside the door.
Aunt Juley You've done this on purpose!
Soames Don't be ridiculous. I did not know what time she was coming.

Irene enters. She looks ravishing. She is much more self-assured. A very different Irene

Hallo, Irene.

Irene Good-day, Soames. Aunt Juley, Aunt Hester?

Aunt Juley Come along, James.

Aunt Juley takes hold of James and practically drags him to the exit

James (*as he goes*) What's she doing here? No-one told me she was coming. But then no-one tells me anything anymore.

Aunt Juley and James exit

Aunt Hester (*holding out her hand*) Hallo, Irene.

Irene (*taking it*) Hester.

Aunt Hester Please excuse them. They're a little ... well ... (*She smiles*) Goodbye, my dear. Good-day, Soames.

Soames Good-day, Aunt.

Aunt Hester leaves

Irene moves downstage looking round the room

Irene Nothing has changed.

Soames I'm sorry you had to face them. I didn't know they were coming. There was a funeral today and I should have been there.

Irene We could have delayed our meeting. Another day would not have made any difference.

Pause. Soames looks at her

Soames You haven't changed either.

Irene Oh, I have. In ways you wouldn't approve of I fear. (*Looking about*) I dreaded coming here but now I have, it doesn't seem to matter. I don't feel anything. (*She turns to look at him*) Why did you send for me?

Soames To discuss certain matters.

Irene I have heard from Cousin Jo what you want from me.

Soames Yes. His return to the fold has proved invaluable to me.

Irene Jo is a good man. A kind man. He has become a close friend, I am pleased to say.

Soames Good. Well?

Irene I am willing to divorce as I have always said.

Soames Then perhaps you will be kind enough to give me the information on which I can act. The law must be complied with.

Irene I have none to give you that I know of.

Soames So I gather from young Jo, but ... after twelve years? Do you really suppose I can believe that?

Irene I do not suppose you will believe anything I say but it is the truth.

Soames (*beat*) I hear you are comfortably off now?

Irene Thank you, yes.

Soames Why didn't you let me provide for you? I would have in spite of everything.

A faint smile crosses Irene's face

You are still my wife, you know.

She doesn't reply. He moves towards her

You had better tell me, Irene. It is to your advantage to be free as well as mine.

Irene I *have* told you.

Soames Do you mean to tell me there has been nothing—nobody?

Irene Nobody. You must look to your own life.

Soames moves away angrily

Soames That won't do. *You* deserted *me*! In common justice it's for you . . .

Irene Why didn't you divorce me then? Do you think I would have cared?

He looks at her

Soames Why couldn't you have made me a good wife?

Irene Yes, it was a crime to marry you and I have paid for it. You will find some way to obtain your divorce I have no doubt. You need not mind my name. I have none to lose. I think I had better go. (*She moves upstage*)

Soames Not yet.

Irene I'd rather not remain.

Soames (*taking a small case from his jacket pocket*) I brought you this. (*He hands her a green moroccan case*) It's for your birthday.

Irene (*refusing*) No thank you.

Soames presses a button and the lid opens to reveal a brooch with seven stones gleaming on pale grey velvet

Soames Take it. As a sign you won't bear me ill feeling.

Irene I couldn't!

Soames (*taking the brooch out of the case*) Let me see how it looks.

Irene shrinks from him. He follows her and presses the brooch against her dress. Shuddering, she moves away

Irene, let bygones be bygones. If *I* can, surely you might. Let us begin again—as if nothing had happened. Won't you?

Irene cannot answer as she stands there dreading him coming nearer to her

Come back to me and I will give you all you want. You shall have your own life. I swear it.

She looks unbelievingly at him

I mean it this time! I'll ask only one thing of you.

Irene No! Not that again, please!

Soames Is it so unnatural to want a child from one's own wife? You wrecked our life and put this blight on to everything. We go on half alive and without any future. Is it so unflattering to you in spite of everything that I still want you for my wife? (*Pause*) Speak! For God's sake say something.

Irene cannot speak

(*Gently*) I don't want to frighten you. Heaven knows I only want you to see that I cannot go on like this. I want you back, Irene.

Irene raises her hand just as Soames moves to her. He stops and her hand covers her mouth. Her eyes never leave him

It's not too late. It's not! If only you'll believe it.

Soames suddenly seizes her hand. She gasps

Irene Don't! (*Then quietly, as he stands there holding her*) I warn you, you will not behave again as you once behaved in this house.

Soames loosens his grip and turns away

Soames (*after a long pause*) I am offering you what few men would bring themselves to offer. I want a reasonable answer.
Irene Reason has nothing to do with it. You can only have the brutal truth. I would rather die!

Soames looks at her, shocked

Soames Oh! (*Then, as if he has received a deadly insult and does not yet know how to deal with it*) Oh, as bad as that. Indeed! You would rather die. That's very pretty.
Irene I'm sorry. You wanted me to answer. I can't help the truth.

Soames snaps the brooch into its case and returns it to his pocket

Soames The truth. There's no such thing with women. I don't believe a word of what you've said. You have a lover. If you hadn't, you wouldn't be such a—a little idiot!

Irene turns away from him again

I meant to do everything I could to do away with the past and start fair again. And all you do is meet me with ... There's nothing tangible is there? It's like a spider's web.
Irene I'm afraid it is, Soames.
Soames Well, I don't choose to be in a spider's web. I'll cut it.

He goes straight to Irene who is fearful of what he is about to do. He embraces and kisses her fully on her tightened lips

Irene (*as he kisses her*) Noooooooooo! (*With utter loathing, she pushes him violently away*)

He stands there for a moment, looking at her. Defiantly, she wipes the kiss off with the back of her hand

Soames turns and walks straight out

The Lights fade to a Black-out

CURTAIN

ACT II

Scene 1

Soames's house in Knightsbridge. January, 1901

The cane settee C *has been replaced by a circular seat*

The Lights come up to full on Aunts Hester and Juley sitting at the table R *with James, looking very solemn. There is a tray of sandwiches and tea on the table*

Aunt Hester An era has passed.
James What's that?
Aunt Juley Hester said: "An era has passed".
James Oh. She had a lot of anxiety, the Queen. She must be glad to be out of it.
Aunt Hester She was a good age.
Aunt Juley Just like a Forsyte.
James It won't be long before I join her.

Pause. No response

(*Disappointedly, looking at them*) *Will it?*
Aunt Juley Don't be morbid, James. You may be deaf and Hester nearly blind, but there's plenty of fight left in us yet.
Aunt Hester Would you like another sandwich, James?
James What?
Aunt Juley She said...
Aunt Hester I may be nearly blind, as you put it, Juley, but I have not been rendered speechless.
James (*quietly*) More's the pity!

Hester, who has heard this remark, glares at him reproachfully

Aunt Hester I said, James: "Would you like another sandwich?"
James No thank you. Don't care much for what's in them.
Aunt Hester What about you, Juley?
Aunt Juley No more for me thank you.
Aunt Hester You know, I often wonder whether it's worthwhile getting old when you see how the world is changing. We're now in the twentieth century with all the promise, so they tell us, of new things, new ways of thinking...
James Family life!
Aunt Juley What?
James What's the matter, Juley? Going deaf? (*He laughs and then coughs*)
Aunt Hester He said, "Family life".
Aunt Juley What about it?

Aunt Hester (*to James*) She said——

James I know what she said thank you, Juley! It's changed.

Aunt Juley *Our* family hasn't changed, James. Only some of the people in it!

James I had hoped for grandchildren to leave my money to. There's only my nephew Val and he's out in South Africa, God knows where. And if I did leave it to him his irresponsible father would no doubt get his hands on it. So what am I left with? A bunch of women. And what sane man would leave his money to them? We all know how women waste a man's money.

Aunt Juley Maybe Soames's new wife, when she makes an appearance, will solve your problem for you.

James Huh! A foreigner! I never thought Soames, of all people, would marry a damn foreigner.

Aunt Juley I suppose anything would be better after *that* woman.

Aunt Hester You can be so cruel at times, Juley. Annette could be very nice.

James How can she be? She's French!

Aunt Juley My dear Hester, if she was *that* nice why did Soames marry her in secret? And in Paris? No-one knew about the wedding—not even his own father here!

James Well, that's par for the course, isn't it? No-one tells me anything so it's all the same to me.

Aunt Hester (*angrily*) If it's all the same to you, James, why do you keep complaining about it?

Aunt Juley looks surprised at Hester's sudden burst of temerity

James I don't see why you should take that tone, Hester. May I remind you that I *am* still head of this family. I'm due some measure of respect, surely?

Aunt Hester Of course you are, James, but I'm sure Soames has his reasons for doing what he did.

James Perhaps you'd care to enlighten me then because I don't understand what's been going on these last few years.

Aunt Hester For heaven's sakes, James, there's been enough publicity over his divorce with Irene. Even *you* must have been aware of this squalid and acrimonious affair.

They freeze as the Lights crossfade to a spotlight L

Soames, Jo and Irene enter the spotlit area

Soames Well? What have you got to say for yourselves?

Jo (*producing a letter*) What we have each received today from your solicitor has taken away your right to ask.

Soames You think so? I tell you that I will divorce her with every circumstance of disgrace, unless you swear to keep clear of one another. Well, Irene?

Irene goes to speak. Jo puts his hand on her arm

Let her alone! Irene! Will you swear it?

Irene No.

Soames (*to Jo*) And you?

Jo Still less.

Soames Then you're guilty, are you?

Irene Yes. Guilty!

Soames (*starting forward*) You devil!

Jo (*interposing*) Get out, Soames! Get out of my house! You are not welcome here.

Soames Call yourself a Trustee! Embezzling Trust property! A thief, stealing his cousin's wife!

Jo Call me what you like. You have chosen your part. We have chosen ours. Now get out.

Soames I'll make you pay!

Jo I shall be very happy.

Soames starts to go, then turns

Soames I only hope you'll treat him as you treated me!

Soames goes

Jo Irene, you had no need to say——

Irene puts her hand to his lips

Irene No, please, Jo. All these months—all these things we haven't said to each other . . .

Jo Irene——

Irene I have come to an end, Jo. If you want me . . . I am here.

The Lights crossfade to R

Irene and Jo leave

James That woman! Don't mention her name. I forbid it!

Aunt Hester I'm sorry. It just slipped out. Anyway, I'm sure Soames was acting in the best interests of the family by not making a public spectacle of his second marriage.

Aunt Juley Not after the public spectacle of his first you mean?

Aunt Hester No, Juley! That is *not* what I mean. I think Soames did the right thing however much we may disapprove.

James A hole-in-the-corner affair.

Aunt Juley And not a member of the family present. I can't remember such a thing happening before. I agree with James.

Aunt Hester What's done is done. Besides we shall be meeting the lady in question in a minute. That's what Soames invited us here for, wasn't it? It's not as if he's completely ignored us.

Aunt Juley (*sarcastically*) Oh, it's very good of Soames, I must say, in allowing us to meet his new wife!

Aunt Hester You're getting bitter in your old age, Juley. I believe Soames acted honourably throughout the whole sordid affair.

Aunt Juley Sordid affair is right. What's more sordid than having to employ a private detective to follow your wife across half of Europe to see how many infidelities she's committing.

Aunt Hester It wasn't half of Europe, Juley. It was Paris.

Aunt Juley The bill Soames received from that detective agency suggests half of Europe—at least! Still, a husband, especially in Soames's position, shouldn't have to have a stranger finding out what his wife is up to when his back's turned. She should be in her proper place—the home.

Aunt Hester You seem to be forgetting the realities of the situation.

Aunt Juley I'm quite aware of the situation.

James The fact remains that if Soames had been the man I brought him up to be, he wouldn't have let it go on for so long. He should have tamed that damn woman and made her see where her loyalty *and* her duty lay.

Aunt Juley I'm sure you're right, James, but as Hester says that's in the past. How do we, as an important family, come to terms with the fact that Irene is now living openly with Young Jo in the house your son built?

James doesn't reply. He acts as if he hasn't heard, and picks up his tea and sips

That's right. You turn a deaf ear when it suits you. When you can't face the realities of life. Just like Hester!

Aunt Hester I don't see there's much to be gained from dwelling on the seamier side of the affair, Juley. Unlike you I can't bring myself to enjoy it.

Aunt Juley I take strong exception to that, Hester. I deal with life as it is, not as we would like it to be. We have to recognize the fact that standards have dropped, even in our lifetime. And now our dear Queen is gone I dread to think what will happen to the world—let alone our beloved Empire! And you can't escape the fact that it's even affected *our* family when one is forced to witness a Forsyte living with a divorced woman and expecting his child! Only June of all people seems to have come out of the mess with some honour. At least she's become a Red Cross nurse!

Aunt Hester Perhaps—"You know who"—and Jo will get married.

Aunt Juley Shutting the stable door after the horse has bolted, wouldn't you say, dear?

Soames enters

Aunt Hester Ah, Soames. There you are.

Soames Hallo, Aunt Hester.

James My boy.

Soames Father. (*He moves to his father and shakes his hand. Then he kisses Aunts Hester and Juley*)

Annette enters during this. She looks somewhat shy and stands by the entrance

Aunt Juley Hallo, Soames.

Soames Aunt Juley.

Soames moves to Annette and, taking her arm, brings her forward

Sorry we've been so long. Father. Aunts. I'd like you to meet my wife. This is Annette.

James How do you do, my dear.

Annette Monsieur.

James Did you have a good journey?

Annette It was all right.

Soames Sit down, Father, please.

James I'm afraid standing tires me out very quickly these days.

James sits

Soames (*to Annette*) This is Aunt Hester.

Aunt Hester Hallo, my dear, and welcome to London.

Annette Thank you.

Soames And this is Aunt Juley. She's not as fierce as she looks.

Aunt Juley You're very pretty. Almost too pretty for Soames.

Soames (*smiling at Annette*) *Sometimes* she's not as fierce as she looks! Would you like some tea, dear?

Annette Thank you. (*She sits*)

Aunt Hester I'll do it, Soames.

Aunt Hester picks up the teapot and Aunt Juley has to guide the pot to the cup as Aunt Hester peers ahead

What do you think of London, Annette?

Annette Oh, I know it already. I have visited many times before.

Aunt Juley Oh? And what part do you know the best?

Annette Soho.

The Aunts look aghast and Aunt Hester misses the cup altogether. James chokes on his cup of tea sending a spray of liquid before him

James (*shocked*) Soho? Did she say Soho?

Soames (*hurriedly*) Er ... yes ... Father. Annette's mother owned a restaurant there. Annette used to help her out on occasions.

Aunt Juley You mean ... you worked?

Annette I did the accounts, yes.

Aunt Juley Well!

Aunt Hester (*trying to be nice*) How exciting! Speaking for myself I've never been very good at adding up.

Juley looks at Hester with disdain

Soames That's where we met.

James Where?

Soames Mrs Lamotte's restaurant, Father.

James One of our properties was it, Soames?

Soames Yes.

James Hope they paid their rent regularly!

Soames raises his eyes helplessly to the sky

Aunt Juley So you didn't meet in France then?
Annette No.
Soames We met in London, Aunt Juley.
Aunt Juley (*heavy with innuendo*) In Soho to be precise, Soames.
Soames (*lightly*) I told you, Annette, to beware of these two. Mischievous they are. Absolutely wicked. They see scandal and mayhem everywhere—even when it doesn't exist.
Aunt Hester Don't you listen to him, Annette. It's just that we've reached a state of advanced years when gossip, even harmless gossip, is all we have left with which to amuse ourselves.

Gentle laughter

Aunt Juley (*to Annette*) Well, you'll find us all a bit strange at first, my dear, but you'll become readily acceptable when you've served your apprenticeship and given Soames a son.
Aunt Hester } (*together*) { *Juley!*
Soames } (*together*) { I do think you might phrase yourself more delicately, Aunt. (*To Annette*) I apologize on behalf of——
Annette That's quite all right, Soames. (*To Juley*) I can't promise anything of course...
Soames Of course she can't. But you can rest assured Annette will shoulder her wifely responsibilities when the time comes.
James Doesn't nature have something to say in the matter?
Aunt Hester Not according to Juley. We Forsytes can dictate terms to nature as well as anyone else.
Annette (*smiling*) Soames is so certain our first born will be a son, aren't you, mon cher? Whereas I... I believe we shall have a daughter.

Black-out

Suddenly we hear some piano music in the style of the twenties

Everyone exits

Scene 2

June's art gallery in Cork Street, May, 1920

A sculpture of a head and shoulders stands on the R *table*

The Light comes up on Fleur, a pretty, vivacious young woman of nineteen, who stands downstage C *looking at some imaginary pictures on the fourth wall. She studies one painting in particular and begins to look at it from every conceivable angle trying to understand it*

After a moment, Michael Mont, who is in his twenties, enters and moves along the row of pictures towards Fleur. As he approaches it can be clearly seen that he finds her more attractive than the art

Sensing his looks she glances straight at Mont who smiles and bows slightly. Then he returns his gaze to the paintings, though his mind isn't on them

Fleur now moves to another painting pretending to be interested. Then she side-glances at Mont and is caught as Mont now looks straight at her. Off balance, she smiles, inclines her head and looks back at the painting in front of her

Mont (*after clearing his throat*) Do you like modern art?
Fleur Er . . . I don't think so.
Mont Admittedly it is an acquired taste.
Fleur Then I doubt whether I shall ever acquire it.
Mont (*moving to her*) My name's Mont.
Fleur (*feigning disinterest*) Is it? How nice.
Mont Michael Mont.

She smiles

Fleur Tell me, Mr Mont. How can you acquire—your word not mine—an appreciation of a painting when you can't for the life of one, tell whether it's hanging upside down or not?

Mont looks at her, then at the painting. He smiles. The smile turns into laughter in which Fleur joins. Mont moves close to her

My name's Fleur. Fleur Forsyte.
Mont I'm pleased to meet you, Miss Forsyte.
Fleur Thank you.
Mont Are you here alone?
Fleur Good heavens no. My father's over there (*indicating off*) talking to the owner of this gallery.
Mont Miss June Forsyte?
Fleur Yes.
Mont Is she a relative?
Fleur Distant, I believe. There are masses of us, I'm afraid. The Forsytes are all over London and the Home Counties.

They both laugh again as they move along to look at another painting

Tell me, Mr Mont. What do you make of this?
Mont (*looking seriously at it*) Mother and Child.
Fleur Exactly.

Mont looks at her questioningly

I mean, where are they? I don't see them.
Mont (*laughing*) You're incorrigible. (*He looks off*) Oh, your father's returning. I hope we'll meet again on some future occasion, Miss Forsyte. Good-day . . .
Fleur You don't have to go . . .

She turns and Mont moves away to exit

Soames enters

Soames Fleur?
Fleur Yes, Father?
Soames Do you know that young man?
Fleur What young man?
Soames I'm not blind. That young man! (*He indicates Mont*)

Mont exits

Fleur Never seen him in my life before.
Soames He gave the impression that he knew you.
Fleur Did he?
Soames I'm not being a busybody, my dear ...
Fleur (*smiling and taking his arm*) I know. You're being a father and that's much worse.
Soames (*smiling*) You wretch! I'm a father who takes his responsibilities seriously, I hope. You can't be too careful these days. Men don't have the same respect for women as they did in my day.
Fleur Father, don't make such a fuss. I'm not a child. In any case didn't I see you speaking to him soon after we arrived?
Soames We happened to be admiring the same painting. He seemed extremely knowledgeable on the subject.
Fleur As knowledgeable as you?
Soames For one so young, yes.
Fleur What painting was it?
Soames Actually, this one. Mother and Child.
Fleur (*trying to disguise a smile*) Oh.
Soames Truly a masterpiece. (*Pause*) He gave me his card.
Fleur Really? (*Playing the innocent*) What's his name?
Soames Didn't he tell you?
Fleur Oh, Daddy, please don't be an ogre.
Soames (*playfully*) Ogre, am I? In that case I definitely won't tell you.

Irene enters with her son, Jon, who is also aged nineteen

They move R *and look at the sculpture and consult the catalogue. Soames cannot see them but Fleur can*

Fleur Does he live in London?
Soames (*taking out a card from his pocket*) Let me see ... Yes. (*Pocketing the card*) His name is Michael Mont and he lives in London. You really are smitten by him, aren't you?
Fleur Of course not. He seemed ... well ... interesting that's all. (*She sees Irene and immediately changes the subject*) Oh, just look at that lady, Father. Isn't she beautiful?
Soames Hm?

Soames turns and stares at Irene. At the same time Jon notices Fleur and stares at her. Irene hasn't seen Soames yet as she is busy concentrating on sculpture

(*Urgently*) We must go.

Fleur But why?
Soames It's—it's getting late. Come along.
Fleur But, Father, we haven't been here five minutes. I'm not going yet.
Soames Please do as I say.

At this point Fleur manages to "accidentally on purpose" drop her handkerchief and begins to make rather a fuss about it

Fleur Oh, dear, now look what I've done.
Soames What's the matter?
Fleur My handkerchief...

Soames is about to stoop and pick it up for her but Jon skilfully gets there instead

Jon Please. Allow me.

Jon picks up the handkerchief and hands it to Fleur who smiles sweetly at him

Fleur Thank you.
Soames Yes, thank you, young man. Come along, my dear.
Fleur (*ignoring Soames*) My name's Fleur Forsyte and this is my father.
Jon Forsyte? That's my name too.
Fleur Really?
Jon I'm Jolyon Forsyte, but everyone calls me Jon.

As the two youngsters start to talk, Soames is looking over at Irene and inwardly hoping that she doesn't see him

Fleur Did you hear that, Father? We have the same name. What fun!
Jon Do you live in London?
Fleur Yes. And you?
Jon We live at Robin Hill, Richmond.
Fleur The country. How lucky you are.

Irene turns to speak to Jon, discovers that he isn't with her and looks across, meeting the eyes of Soames. She is shocked and tries to recover her composure

Is it a big house?
Jon Sort of.
Fleur Father?

Soames doesn't respond

Father?
Soames Er ... yes?
Fleur Could we possibly be related do you think?
Soames Er ... what are you talking about?
Fleur Mr Forsyte and us. Could we be related? We both have the same name...

Soames looks across the room and sees Irene move away

Soames I doubt it ... er ... perhaps. I really don't know.
Fleur Wouldn't it be jolly if we were?

Jon I'd say.
Soames Distant cousins, perhaps.
Jon Really, sir?
Fleur Do you think so, Father?
Soames It's possible. I don't know.
Jon Jolyon Forsyte? Robin Hill?

Having recovered, Soames now stares at the young man with distaste

Soames Cousins. Yes. Distant. Very distant. (*Then dismissively*) Good-day, sir.

Soames takes Fleur's arm and they move off

Jon is left looking after them. Irene, seeing that her son is now alone, moves to him

Irene Jon dear?
Jon Do you know them, Mother?
Irene Know whom, dear?
Jon Did you not see? Fleur Forsyte and her father.
Irene Oh?
Jon He said we could be distant cousins. For some reason I don't think he liked me.

The Lights fade to half

Jon exits

Irene moves L *and sits*

Young Jo enters and stands by her

SCENE 3

Jo's and Irene's house at Robin Hill. Later the same day

Jo notices that Irene seems deep in thought

Jo What is it, Irene?
Irene We had an encounter today.
Jo Oh? Who with?
Irene Soames.

Jo is taken aback and moves away

He and his daughter were at the opening of June's gallery in Cork Street. Afterwards we met again at the confectioners where we had tea.

Jo moves back to her seeing that she can talk about Soames dispassionately

Jo How did he look?
Irene Grey. Otherwise the same.
Jo And the daughter?
Irene Pretty. At least . . .

Jo Yes?
Irene Jon obviously thought so. (*She looks at Jo*)
Jo I see. (*Pause*) You didn't...?
Irene No, of course not. But Jon knows their name. The girl dropped her handkerchief and he picked it up. It was all very queer and strained and Jon could see it was.

Pause

Jo I've often wondered whether it was right to keep it from him. He'll find out some day.
Irene The later the better, Jo. The young have such cheap, hard judgement. When you were nineteen what would you have thought of your mother if she had done what I have?
Jo If I'd known what I know about you and Soames I hope I would have been forgiving.
Irene Jo dear, you're so good to me and I do love you.
Jo And, in the end, that's what it comes down to. Love. True love. It's a very difficult emotion to control. Sometimes it makes us behave quite irrationally.
Irene Yes. It makes us break out, doesn't it? It gives us wings?
Jo For us it did. (*Pause*) What if...?
Irene Yes?
Jo It must have crossed your mind. Jon and ... what's her name?
Irene Fleur. It's an impossible thought.
Jo But it has crossed your mind. What have you told him?
Irene That we were related but we didn't actually know them. That you had never cared for the family, or they for you. I expect he will be asking you about them.

Jo looks at Irene dreading the thought

We've known it would happen some day.
Jo Yes.
Irene And there's something else.
Jo Oh?
Irene Fleur's also been invited to Holly's place the same time as Jon.
Jo Next weekend? How could Holly be so stupid?
Irene She's young. She's not been touched by family intolerance.
Jo So they'll have at least two days there together?
Irene I'm afraid so.
Jo I'll speak to Jon as soon as possible. I could never stand him blaming you for what happened. He shan't do that. Even in thought. He has imagination and he'll understand if it's put to him properly. I think I'd better tell him before he gets to know from other sources.
Irene Please, Jo. Not yet.
Jo That's just like you, my dear. You never go to meet trouble, do you?
Irene That's because trouble always seems to come to me. Maybe if we took Jon away for a few weeks. Abroad. We could go to Spain. A holiday.
Jo (*thinking*) We could try. I'll write to Holly and tell her that Jon knows

nothing of the family history. I'll tell her to be discreet. All right, my dear. Who am I to go against a mother's instinct?

The Lights crossfade to C

Jo and Irene exit. Jo enters C, *casually, hands in pockets, looking around*

SCENE 4

Holly's house in the country. A week later

The sound of birdsong can be heard under the following. After a moment, Fleur can be heard calling

Fleur (*off*) Jon! Jon!
Jon (*calling back*) I'm here.
Fleur (*off*) Where's here?
Jon The conservatory. (*He sits down on the* C *seat*)

Fleur enters

Fleur Oh, there you are. Val and Holly want to know if you're game for a walk?
Jon Where to?
Fleur Across the Downs.
Jon After the lunch we've just had?
Fleur That's the whole idea, silly.
Jon What is?
Fleur To walk it off. Say you'll come.
Jon (*indicating her shoes*) You can't walk across the Downs in those.
Fleur They have a selection of proper walking shoes for reluctant guests. All sizes!
Jon (*glumly*) Val and Holly think of everything don't they?
Fleur Yes, I'm afraid they do. (*She laughs*)
Jon All right then. When do you want to leave?
Fleur In about half an hour.
Jon Oh, that's all right then.
Fleur Why?
Jon Gives me time to summon up some stamina.
Fleur Jon Forsyte, you're the laziest man I've ever met.

They laugh

Jon I hope you haven't met too many men.
Fleur Oh, I have. Lots.
Jon Any that ... interested you?
Fleur (*teasingly*) Dozens!
Jon (*deflated*) Oh.
Fleur (*beat*) But not as interesting as you.
Jon (*brightening*) Really?
Fleur Of course.

Jon Come and sit down beside me, Fleur.
Fleur We're supposed to be going for a walk.
Jon Not for half an hour.

Fleur comes and sits beside Jon. Pause. They look at one another awkwardly and they smile. They freeze

The Lights quickly crossfade to R *where Soames and Annette are in conversation*

Soames What was that you said? About Fleur and Jon Forsyte?
Annette Spending the weekend together, you mean?
Soames (*shocked*) Spending the weekend together?
Annette (*laughing*) Not alone, Soames. At Val and Holly's. An invitation.
Soames You knew of this?
Annette Yes.
Soames How did you know?
Annette June told me. She had also been invited but could not go.
Soames And you said nothing?
Annette Does it matter then?
Soames Of course it matters. You know my wishes.
Annette Some small family quarrel. Yes, you told me.
Soames *No!* Not small! Do my wishes not count, madam?
Annette I believe our daughter's happiness comes first.
Soames What has her happiness to do with it?
Annette She is infatuated with the boy. One can see it when she speaks of him.
Soames They have only met once to my knowledge.
Annette It only takes one spark to kindle a fire.
Soames And you encourage these feelings?
Annette Neither encourage or discourage, Soames. She is a woman like me.
Soames I smell a conspiracy here. You did this deliberately. To get at me.
Annette To get at you?
Soames *Yes!* You and your liberal ideas! That's where Fleur gets her rebellious nature from.
Annette What is all this about? Fleur is visiting her cousin. That is all.
Soames She is seeing a man of whom I whole-heartedly disapprove.
Annette I'm afraid I do not understand. What have you against this boy?
Soames You don't have to understand.
Annette She is my daughter, too.
Soames Then it's time you acted like a responsible mother.
Annette How dare you when I ... (*She stops*)
Soames (*challengingly*) Yes?
Annette No matter.
Soames You have a duty to me as your husband and to Fleur as your daughter.
Annette Is that all?
Soames All? What do you mean?
Annette *Your* wife. *Fleur's* mother. Is that all I'm allowed to be?

Soames For many women that would be enough. And I would remind you that you have another advantage.
Annette Oh? And what is that?
Soames You are also a Forsyte. That means certain privileges and certain responsibilities.
Annette Everything neatly in it's place, eh Soames? Including me.
Soames I don't know what you are suggesting. You are free to come and go as you please providing you remember who you are.
Annette I can hardly fail to do that. And that is why I feel trapped.
Soames Trapped? Trapped? You have more freedom than most.
Annette And you have had what you wanted from me. That is clear.
Soames How dare you!
Annette When Fleur was born our marriage should have ended there. Clearly it ended for you.
Soames You are talking nonsense.
Annette Am I? After Fleur was born I ceased to exist for you.
Soames I think you'd better leave.
Annette That's what you and all the Forsytes cannot stand, isn't it? The great Forsyte family cannot face the truth. Not about themselves. Not about life. Everything must be hidden away for the sake of appearances. For the family name! What hypocrites you all are.
Soames (*losing his temper*) *That is enough!*

Annette shrinks from Soames's blazing anger. Soames suddenly becomes self-conscious

I'm going to my club.

Soames stalks out

Annette freezes

The Lights crossfade to Jon and Fleur sitting C, *smiling at one another*

The sound of birdsong is heard under the following

Jon What are you smiling at?
Fleur Val and Holly actually.
Jon Why?
Fleur At the way they've been manoeuvring us about the place. Like pieces on a chessboard.
Jon Have they?
Fleur You must have noticed, surely! They've taken every opportunity imaginable to get us alone together.
Jon Oh, that.
Fleur Then you have noticed?
Jon Hard not to.
Fleur I think it's rather nice actually. They've been married all this time and they're still incurably romantic.
Jon Is that a bad thing?

During the following, Jon manages to get his arm around Fleur

Fleur I wasn't criticizing. I think it's rather sweet. In fact when I arrived and they introduced us I didn't have the heart to tell them we'd already met in case it spoiled everything for them.

Jon I wondered why you didn't say anything.

Fleur Mind you, they may have already known. News travels fast in this family.

Jon Does it?

Fleur Jon my dear, don't you know *anything*? Mind you, I suppose your branch of the family isn't so much in the thick of things as ours.

Jon What do you mean?

Fleur You don't know about the feud, then?

Jon What feud?

Fleur Between our families. Personally, I find it all rather romantic—romantic *and* silly. (*Suddenly noticing his arm around her*) Do you do this often?

Jon (*nervously removing his arm*) Do you mind, then?

Fleur (*laughing*) I'm only teasing. (*She suddenly stops laughing and becomes serious*)

Jon What's the matter?

Fleur They'll put a stopper on us, you know.

Jon What do you mean?

Fleur (*playfully imitating him*) "What do you mean? What do you mean?" Once they find out we've been together, silly!

Jon Does it matter?

Fleur You really *don't* know what's going on, do you? Mind you, you can't get anyone to speak about it openly and honestly. Even Holly wouldn't talk about it when I asked her.

Jon You asked her?

Fleur Of course. How do you know what's going on if you don't ask. You're terribly old fashioned if you don't mind me saying so.

Jon As old fashioned as dropping your handkerchief on purpose in the art gallery?

Fleur Oh, dear. Was it that obvious?

Jon A bit. Still, I liked you for it.

Fleur It was all I could think of at the time. I think your mother's incredibly beautiful, by the way.

Jon Yes, isn't she?

Fleur I love all things of beauty—when it's exciting . . .

Fleur suddenly becomes aware that while she's been talking Jon has been staring adoringly at her. She stops and returns his gaze for a moment

(*Finally*) Of all the things in the world, don't you think caution is the most awful?

Slowly they move closer together. Their lips meet in a gently, lingering kiss. They freeze

The Lights crossfade to Irene and Soames who are in conversation

Soames I had to see you.

Irene We have nothing to say.

Soames Not even when it comes to our respective offspring?

Irene You need to speak to Jolyon.

Soames I need to speak to you!

Irene Why?

Soames Because ... (*He looks at her suddenly as if to say "because I wanted to see you again". He quickly changes tack*) Because I think you have conspired with my daughter ...

Irene Conspired?

Soames That's what I said. Conspired to——

Irene I said I never wanted to see you again, Soames, and I would prefer it if you honoured my wish.

Soames I had to come here on a matter which concerns us closely. And I want to know exactly what part you have played in it.

Irene I don't know what you're talking about.

Soames You don't? You know nothing of the fact that at this moment your son and my daughter are together at Val and Holly's ...?

Irene Oh ...

Soames Yes, madam. "Oh." You knew about it, then?

Irene Of course.

Soames And your husband too?

Irene Yes.

Soames I see. Everyone knew except me it seems ...

Irene Four young people spending the weekend together. What harm is there in that?

Soames It seems that common decency doesn't mean anything any more.

Irene (*angrily*) Common decency? What do you, of all people, know of common decency?

Soames You're not saying you do, I hope, when your past——

Irene I think you had better leave before we say things we shall regret.

Soames Haven't we said them already?

Irene I regret nothing, Soames. Now please go.

Soames I cannot go until I have your promise not to allow your son to see my daughter ever again.

Irene I cannot promise that.

Soames But you must! Fleur is young and easily led ...

Irene My son won't lead her anywhere! While I am in agreement that nothing would cause me more distress than to see our respective children become ... interested in one another, I am not a jailer and I refuse to dictate to my son what he should do and whom he should see.

Soames And does your husband subscribe to this view?

Irene Ask him. He is not here at the moment but I can make an appointment for you to see him ...

Soames Don't treat me like some tradesman, madam! I came here in both our interests.

Irene But not in the interests of our children! That's where we differ, Soames, you and I. I believe they should make up their own minds about whom they should cultivate and yes, whom they should love. It doesn't matter what other, less liberated people think, as long as they are happy. As long as they wake up each morning knowing they have done the right thing by themselves and those they love. (*She looks at Soames for a brief moment*) You don't understand, do you, Soames? You have no idea what I'm talking about. I'm talking about the heart, emotions...

Soames (*distastefully*) I know all about the heart and emotions!

Irene (*shaking her head*) No you don't. You know only one thing. How to make a profit. How to be a Forsyte.

Pause

Soames You have not changed.

Irene Had you expected me to?

Soames I didn't expect you to have any regard for me but my daughter...

Irene Your daughter is in no danger—except from you.

Soames You go too far, Irene.

Irene Fleur is a free spirit, Soames. You may not like it but you can't alter it. For all I know she may love you as much as you obviously love her, but you risk losing her if you try and crush that spirit. Your strength is in letting others fly, Soames, not clipping their wings.

Soames stares at Irene for a moment, then he turns and leaves

Irene freezes as the Lights crossfade to C *where Fleur and Jon sit kissing. They break. There is a long pause. The sound of birdsong is heard under the following*

Fleur You're frightfully silent. I like silence when it's quick. (*She moves away suddenly. Playfully*) I'm disappointed in you, Jon Forsyte.

Jon Oh? Why?

Fleur If you had been a true gentleman you wouldn't have let on that you knew I'd dropped my handkerchief on purpose. You should have continued with the game.

Jon Is that all it is then? A game?

Fleur (*suddenly serious*) No. (*She changes tack*) Daddy nearly died when you picked it up.

Jon Because of this feud thing?

Fleur I don't know. Probably. They've been going at it for years. I intend to get to the bottom of it one way or the other. When I really want something and I put my mind to it, I usually get it, you know.

Jon I suppose your father's fearfully fond of you and protective?

Fleur Yes. I'm an only child, you see. And so are you, at least on your mother's side. Isn't it a bore? There's so much expected of one.

Jon And life's so short. One wants to live forever and know everything.

Fleur And love everyone.

Jon No!

Fleur No?

Jon I only want to love once...

They look at one another again. He takes her hand and kisses it

Fleur Tell me, Jon. Are you a good liar?
Jon Awful. Why?
Fleur Because it's serious about the feud. We've simply got to keep it secret if we want to be together.
Jon (*a thought striking him*) Good Lord!
Fleur What's the matter?
Jon I think you're right.
Fleur About what?
Jon It just occurred to me. I think my parents are already reacting to our meeting at the gallery. Mother said she was taking me to Spain for a holiday when I get back.
Fleur There, I told you. It's started then.

The Lights fade to half

Jon exits. Soames enters

Fleur moves to join Soames R. *The Lights come up to full*

Scene 5

Soames's house in Knightsbridge. Three weeks later

Soames I couldn't believe it, Fleur.
Fleur It was all terribly harmless, Daddy.
Soames Harmless? You spend a weekend in the country with your cousin...
Fleur About which you knew...
Soames Yes, but I didn't know that ... *he'd* be there!
Fleur What difference does it make?
Soames The son of ... well ... never mind. You say "harmless". Much you know of what's harmless and what isn't.

Fleur sighs

Fleur (*calmly*) Well then, dear, suppose you tell me and be quite frank about it.

Soames looks at her for a moment and then sits beside her

Soames You're my only comfort and you go away and do something like that.
Fleur Like what, dear?
Soames You know what I told you. I don't choose to have anything to do with that branch of the family.
Fleur Yes, dear, but I don't know *why* I shouldn't.
Soames (*getting up*) I'm not going into reasons. You ought to trust me.

Fleur looks down, swinging her leg with some anger

You know my wishes! I suppose that boy travelled back with you.
Fleur (*angrily*) *Jon!* Father. His name is Jon!

Fleur looks at Soames challengingly. This makes Soames a little uneasy

Soames This is not an inquisition, Fleur, even though you may think it is.
Fleur (*getting up*) Will it make you any happier if I promise not to see him for say . . . the next six weeks? That's how long he's going to be in Spain. Six whole weeks.
Soames (*angrily*) Six weeks? Six years? Sixty years more like. Don't delude yourself, Fleur. Don't dare delude yourself.
Fleur (*taken back by her father's vehemence*) Father? What it is?

Soames moves to her

Soames Don't tell me that you're foolish enough to have any feelings beyond caprice? That would be too much.
Fleur Then it is deep. (*Taking his arm*) No, of course. Caprice. Only, I like my caprices better than I like yours.
Soames Mine! (*He moves away*)
Fleur Father, I know about this feud of yours.
Soames Feud? What feud?
Fleur I saw June. We talked about it. Admittedly she didn't want to, but I persisted.
Soames June! What does she know? A first cousin removed.
Fleur But the daughter of your enemy.
Soames What do you mean by that?
Fleur I beg your pardon. I thought he was.
Soames Enemy? It's ancient history. I don't know where you get your notion.
Fleur I told you. From June Forsyte.

Soames looks at her

Soames If, as you say, you know, why do you plague me?
Fleur I don't want to plague you, darling.
Soames *That chap*! (*He turns and looks out. He has ended the conversation*)
Fleur Am I dismissed?

Soames doesn't reply

A Maid enters suddenly

Miad Excuse me, Miss Fleur.
Fleur Yes?
Maid A Mr Mont is here to see you.
Fleur I'll be out in a moment.

The Maid exits

Soames He called two or three times while you were away.
Fleur He's more the man you'd like to have for a son-in-law, isn't he, Father?
Soames Son-in-law? Has it got to that then?
Fleur No. Jon and I have only met on two occasions and you were with me on the first you may remember.

Soames And I also remember you were smitten by him and he by you. And young people allow their emotions to run fast, not like in my day.

Pause. Fleur doesn't reply but moves to the exit

Fleur?
Fleur Yes, Father?
Soames Do you like him?
Fleur Who?
Soames Mont of course!
Fleur (*after a pause*) Yes. He's rather nice.

Fleur exits

Soames stands there for a moment

Soames Nice! Only for the next six weeks, no doubt!

The Lights crossfade to L

Soames exits

Scene 6

Jo's and Irene's house at Robin Hill. Several weeks later

Jon sits L *in a chair snoozing*

Fleur enters and, seeing him asleep, kisses him on the nose playfully

Jon Fleur! What are you doing?
Fleur Your parents told me you were here. I didn't think they would, knowing who I am. But they were charming.
Jon What are you talking about, you idiot! (*He gets up and kisses her*)
Fleur You haven't forgotten me then after six weeks abroad?
Jon How could I? What about you? Has anyone cut in yet?
Fleur There *is* a young idiot, but it doesn't count. How was Spain?
Jon All right. I had sunstroke. I didn't tell you.
Fleur Was it interesting?
Jon No. Mother was an angel though.
Fleur I've found out what's happened between our families.
Jon Do tell.

They sit down together

Fleur I believe my father wanted to marry your mother but your father got her instead. I came upon a photo of her. It was in the frame behind a photo of me. Of course, if Father was very fond of her, that would make him pretty mad, wouldn't it?
Jon (*pause*) Not if she loved my father best.
Fleur But suppose they were engaged?
Jon If we were engaged and you found somebody better, I might go cracked, but I shouldn't grudge it you.

Fleur Well, I should. *You* mustn't ever do that to me, Jon.
Jon Not a hope.
Fleur I don't believe my father ever really cared for my mother.
Jon Honestly?
Fleur It's a feeling I have when they're together—which isn't very often. I don't know, I always get the impression that the Forsyte women are permanently chained down.
Jon It's a sense of property which makes people chain things down. The older generation thought of nothing else but property. That's why there was a war.
Fleur That never occurred to me. How clever of you. Your people and mine quarrelled over property. I don't know why. We've all got it—at least I suppose your people have.
Jon Yes, luckily. Mind you, I don't suppose I shall be any good at making money.
Fleur If you were I don't believe I should like you.
Jon Like me? Only like me?

They smile at one another and slowly they kiss

(*Taking her hand*) Come on.
Fleur Where are we going?
Jon We're going to make it official.
Fleur Make what official?
Jon The fact that I'm madly in love with you.

The Lights fade down to half

Fleur rushes off. Irene enters and sits L

Jon moves down to join Irene

Scene 7

The same. A few weeks later

The Lights come up on Jon sitting at Irene's feet. The room is flooded in moonlight and they are looking straight ahead into the garden

Irene Those cypresses your grandfather planted when he lived here have done wonderfully well. I always think they look more beautiful in the moonlight than they do by day. (*Beat*) I wish you'd known your grandfather, Jon.
Jon Were you married to Father when he was alive?
Irene No, dear. He died out there, under the oak tree. He was very old; eighty-five, I think. He was extraordinarily kind to me when others ... well ... when others were not so kind. He was very generous and understanding.
Jon Is Father like him?
Irene A little but more subtle and not so solid. But your father has all his other qualities.

Pause

Jon (*taking his mother's hand*) Tell me about the family quarrel, Mother.

Irene stiffens a little. Pause

Irene No, dear. That's for your father when he thinks fit.
Jon Then it was serious?
Irene Yes.

There is a silence between them. Neither knows which turning to take in this conversation

(*Kindly*) Spain didn't help, did it?
Jon You mean the real reason we went?
Irene You guessed, then?
Jon It was pretty obvious.
Irene Was it? I'm sorry. Did you resent it?
Jon I did at first but when I realized your plan wasn't going to work I was determined to enjoy myself.
Irene (*smiling*) You little beast! And there I was thinking how clever we were being.
Jon I suppose you had your reasons.
Irene Yes, darling, we did and you'll understand it all when the time comes for you to know the truth. Not gossip or rumour but the truth.

Pause. They continue staring out at the garden

You love her?
Jon Yes. (*Pause*) Are you angry?
Irene Angry that two people are in love? No. How can one be angry about something like that?
Jon I don't know. It seems to have upset a lot of people in the family when it happened before—all those years ago.

Jon feels Irene draw away. His remark has obviously struck a deep, painful chord

I'm sorry, Mother. I shouldn't have said that. I'd better go to bed. It's been a long day.

Jon gets up and kisses Irene on the cheek

Irene Good-night, darling.
Jon Good-night, Mother.

Jon leaves

Irene stares out

After a moment, Jo comes in and sits down beside her

Irene Spain was a complete waste of time.
Jo I thought it might be.
Irene He's in love with her.

Jo Oh.

She puts her arm through his

Irene I'm afraid, Jo.
Jo You must let me tell him, Irene, and have done with it. After all, Jon has the instincts of a gentleman. He has only to understand——
Irene Only? He can't understand. It's impossible.
Jo I believe I could have, at his age.
Irene You were always more the realist than Jon. And never so innocent.
Jo That's true. It's queer, isn't it? You and I would tell our story to the world without a particle of shame but our own boy stumps us.
Irene That's because we've never cared whether the world approves of us or not.
Jo Jon wouldn't disapprove of us, would he?
Irene Oh, yes Jo, he would. That's what frightens me. He's in love. He's said so. And he'd say: "My mother once married without love. How could she have?" It would seem to him a crime. (*Pause*) And so it was.
Jo (*taking her hand in his*) Why on earth are we born young? Hm? If only we were born old and grew younger year by year we should understand how things happen and stop being intolerant. (*Pause*) I'm afraid nothing will really cure him, Irene, but the shock of being told.

She looks sadly at him

Irene I know.

Jo kisses her gently

Jo I love you, dear, dear Irene.

The Lights crossfade to R

Jo and Irene exit

Scene 8

Soames's house in Knightsbridge. A few weeks later

Michael Mont is in the room

Soames enters after a moment

Soames Please sit down, Mont.
Mont I thought Fleur would have been back, sir. But I'm glad she isn't. The fact is ... I ... I'm fearfully gone on her. In fact I'm so fearfully gone on her I thought you'd better know. It's old fashioned of course, coming to the father first but I thought you'd forgive that. I went to my own dad and he says if I settle down he'll see me through. He rather cottons to the idea in fact.
Soames Oh? He rather cottons?
Mont Yes, sir. Do you?

Soames smiles faintly

You see, when you've been through the war you can't help being in a hurry.

Soames To get married and unmarried, you mean?

Mont Not from Fleur, sir.

Soames My daughter's too young.

Mont Oh, no sir. We're awfully old nowadays. That's why I must hang around or I won't have a dog's chance. You'll let Fleur do what she likes, I suppose?

Soames Mr Mont. You may think you're very old but you strike me as extremely young. To rattle ahead of everything is not proof of your maturity.

Mont All right, sir. But I want you to know how serious I am about your daughter. I've got myself a job.

Soames I'm pleased to hear it.

Mont I've joined a publisher. My father's putting up the stakes.

Soames I don't dislike you, Mr Mont——

Mont Thank you, sir.

Soames Allow me to finish.

Mont Sorry, sir.

Soames As I was saying; I don't dislike you but Fleur means everything to me. Everything. Do you understand?

Mont Yes, sir. I know. But so she does to me.

Soames That's as maybe. I'm glad you've told me of your feelings towards my daughter, however. And now I think there's nothing more to be said.

Mont I know it rests with her, sir.

Soames It will rest with her a long time, I hope.

The door opens and Annette enters

Annette I'm sorry I——

Soames That's all right, my dear. Mr Mont is just leaving. Good-night, Mont.

Mont I really do think an awful lot of her, sir.

Soames Yes, I do understand. Good-night.

Mont Good-night, sir. (*As he passes Annette*) Good-night, madame.

Mont exits

Soames (*sighing heavily*) The younger generation. (*He sits down*)

Annette You asked to see me.

Soames Over an hour ago, yes.

Annette I had other things to do.

Soames Other things . . . I see. (*Pause. He takes a torn letter from his pocket*) I've had this. (*He holds it up*)

Annette What is it?

Soames Take it. Read it.

She reluctantly takes it from him. She moves away reading it

Annette It's dirty! Filthy!

Soames I agree. Degrading even. Is it true?
Annette (*turning to face him; brazenly*) And what if it were?
Soames Is that all you have to say?
Annette No.
Soames Well? Speak out!
Annette What is the good of talking?
Soames (*icily*) So you admit it!
Annette I admit nothing. You are a fool to ask. A man like you should not ask. It is dangerous.

Soames gets up and moves towards her

Soames Do you remember what you were when I married you? Working in a restaurant.
Annette Don't look down on me, Soames. Remember this too. I was not half your age!
Soames (*moves away*) I am not going to bandy words. I require you to give up this ... friendship. I think of the matter entirely as it affects Fleur.
Annette Ah, Fleur. Of course. Always Fleur.
Soames She's your child as well as mine.
Annette Oh! It is kind of you to admit it.
Soames Are you going to do as I say?
Annette I refuse to tell you.
Soames Then I must make you.
Annette (*smiling*) No, Soames. You are helpless.

Soames goes to speak

Do not say things you'll regret! There will be no more letters. I promise. When two people have married and lived like us they had better be quiet about each other. There are things one does not drag into the light for other people to laugh at. You will be quiet, not for my sake but for your own.
Soames You are a bad woman who opens the bedroom door to me when it suits her.
Annette Because, Soames, you regard me more as a mistress than a wife! Living with you has killed things in me. Let me remind you of something, Soames. Do you remember the day you heard your father was dying? The same day as Fleur was born. And the doctor came to you and told you he needed to operate to save my life, but in operating he couldn't guarantee the life of our child?
Soames Why drag that up? You were both delivered safely.
Annette You wanted a son so much you *refused* permission for that operation to take place even though it meant endangering my life. That's how much you thought of me. That's how much you thought of our marriage. When, later, I heard what you'd done, something died in me there and then. I could never forgive you.

They look at one another. A long pause

Look at yourself. You are getting old. And I am not yet old. You see, Soames, living with you has made me very practical.

Pause

Soames I require you to give up this friendship.
Annette And if I don't?
Soames Then—then I will cut you out of my will.

Annette laughs

I shall see this man and warn him off.

Annette Mon cher, you are funny. You do not want me. You have as much of me as you need and you wish the rest of me to be dead. I admit nothing but I am not going to be dead, not at my age, so you had better be quiet. I myself will make no scandal. I am saying no more.

Soames You! (*Beat*) You are just like ... Irene! Strong willed. But I never realized *how* strong.

Annette The trouble with you, Soames, is you know nothing about women and even less about love.

Annette exits

The Lights crossfade to L

Scene 9

Jo's and Irene's house at Robin Hill. Several weeks later

Jo is sitting in an armchair, snoozing. He looks old and ill

Jon enters. He smiles at his father and then goes to him and kisses his forehead. Jo stirs

Jo Jon, my boy. Where did you spring from?
Jon I came to tell you something, Dad.
Jo (*suspecting*) I see ... Well, sit down, old man. Have you seen your mother?
Jon No. (*Nervous, he sits on the edge of the chair*)
Jo (*leaning forward*) Well?
Jon Fleur and I are engaged.

Jo leans back in the chair with a heavy sigh. During the following, his breathing becomes fatigued and his hand wavers over his chest

(*Getting up and moving away*) I know that you and Mother don't like the idea. Fleur says that Mother was engaged to her father before you married her. Of course, I don't know what happened, but it must have been years ago. I'm devoted to Fleur, Dad, and she says she's devoted to me.

Jo You are nineteen, Jo, and I am seventy-two. How are we to understand each other in a matter like this?

Jon (*turning and moving back to his father*) You love Mother, Dad. You must know what we feel. It isn't fair to us to let old things spoil our happiness, is it?

Jo (*laying his hand on his arm*) Look, Jon. I could try and put you off with talk about you both being too young and all that, but you wouldn't listen. *You* talk lightly of "old things" knowing nothing of what actually happened. My dear boy, have I ever given you reason to doubt my love for you. Or my word?

Jon looks at his father, shakes his head and sits back in the chair

Very well. You can believe what I tell you, then. (*Beat*) If—if you don't give up this love affair, you will make your mother wretched to the end of her days. Believe me, the past can't be buried. It can't, Jon!

Jon And I can't give her up, Dad. I can't give her up because you say that.

Jo If you knew the story you would give this up without hestiation. You would have to. Can't you believe that?

Jon How can you tell me what I should think? Father, I love her more than anything else in the world.

Jo takes a deep breath as pain strikes his chest

Jo (*after a pause*) Better, my dear boy, than your mother?

The two men look at one another and Jon gets up and moves away

Jon (*with anguish*) I don't know. *I don't know!* To give up Fleur for something I don't fully understand, for something that I don't believe matters half as much as our love for one another is ... impossible!! You want me to trust you, Father. But why don't you trust *me*? We wouldn't want to know anything of the past. We wouldn't let it make any difference. It'll only succeed in making us love you and Mother all the more.

Pause. Jo puts his hand inside his jacket pocket as if to bring out something but he thinks better of it

Jo Think of what your mother's been to you, Jon. She has nothing but you. (*Beat*) I shan't last much longer...

Jon (*angrily*) Why not? It isn't fair of you ... (*He stops suddenly and looks at his father's ashen face*) Father? Why not?

Jo (*coldly*) Because the doctors tell me I shan't, that's all.

Pause. Their eyes meet. Jon then moves to his father and kneels by his chair

Jon Oh, Dad... (*He breaks down and weeps*)

Jo (*placing his hand on Jon's head, with tears in his eyes*) Don't ... Please, Jon, don't. (*Pause. Whispering*) Please...

After a moment, Jon gets up and, wiping away the tears, turns away from his father

Don't mention it to your mother, by the way. She has enough to frighten her with this affair of yours. (*Beat*) I know how you feel, Jon. But you know her and me well enough to be sure we wouldn't wish to spoil your happiness lightly. We don't care for anything but your happiness and I for your mother's happiness.

Jon turns to his father again

Jon (*almost a whisper*) Then what is it? What is it, Father? Please don't keep me like this.

Jo looks again at his son. He then reaches out into the inside pocket of his jacket and brings out an envelope

Jo I wanted to spare you. I wanted to spare your mother and myself but I see it's no good. I have written it down. All of it. As it happened. Read it. It will tell you everything you want to know.

Jon takes the envelope

(*Going to get up*) I'll go into the garden.
Jon No, Father. I'll go.

Jon hurries off with the envelope

Exhausted, Jo slumps back into the chair lies back as another pain strikes. He closes his eyes

Jo Dear God ... so ... so it's to be like this, is it?

The Lights slowly fade to a Black-out. A sombre music link takes us into the next scene

SCENE 10

The same. Two weeks later

The Lights come up on Soames sitting waiting nervously

After a moment Irene enters in mourning

Soames stands and looks at her

Soames My God! It's like seeing you for the first time. You were dressed in black then. You were in mourning for your father, I seem to remember.
Irene Won't you sit down?
Soames I ... I'm sorry. I apologize for coming but this business between your son and my daughter must be killed one way or the other. (*He looks at her. Pause*) I've—I've done my best to discourage it. I consider my daughter crazy, but I've got into the habit of indulging her. That's why I'm here. I suppose you're fond of your son?
Irene Devoted.
Soames Well?
Irene It rests with him.
Soames It's a mad notion.
Irene It is.

Pause

Soames If—if you had only ... well ... they might have been ...

Irene, knowing what Soames is about to say, turns away. He notices her expression and moves away

So far as I'm concerned you may put your mind at rest. I desire to see neither you nor your son if this marriage comes about. Young people in these days are ... unaccountable. But I can't bear to see my daughter unhappy. (*Beat*) What am I to say to her when I go back?

Irene Please say to her as I said to you. That it rests with Jon.

Soames You don't oppose it?

Irene Yes. With all my heart. But not with my lips.

He turns to face her

Soames Where is your son?

Irene Upstairs.

Soames Perhaps you'd have him come down, please.

Irene gets up and goes to the exit R

Irene (*calling off*) Jon!

Soames begins to pace nervously. Irene glances at him and then returns to her chair

Soames If it rests with him I suppose I may take it for granted that this unnatural marriage will take place. In that case there will be formalities to go through. Whom do I deal with? Your usual solicitor?

Irene nods

Soames You don't propose to live with them?

Irene No.

Soames What happens to this house?

Irene It will be as Jon wishes.

Soames (*looking about*) This house ... I had hopes when I began it ... such hopes. If *they* live in it ... their children ... They say there's such a thing as Nemesis. Do you believe in it?

Irene Yes.

Soames Oh, you do ...? (*He moves nearer to her*) I'm not likely to see you again. Will you shake hands and—and let the past die? (*He holds out his hand*)

Irene keeps her hands clasped in her lap. She looks at him

Jon enters

Soames turns

Well, young man. I'm here for my daughter. It rests with you it seems. This matter. Your mother leaves it in your hands.

Jon, who has been grief stricken by his father's death, looks at his mother briefly. Soames now stands between them

It is for my daughter's sake that I am here. What am I to say to her when I return?

Jon (*after a moment*) Tell Fleur that I must do as my father wished before his death.
Irene Jon please . . .
Jon It's all right, Mother.

Soames looks from Irene to Jon

Soames That's that then.

Soames exits without another word

The Lights fade to a Black-out

Scene 11

Soames's house in Knightsbridge. Three months later

Suddenly we hear the "Wedding March". Slowly the exit C *is spotlit*

Fleur in a wedding dress and Michael Mont in a morning suit enter from either side of C *opening. Together, they walk arm in arm downstage and then turn to face each other as Mont places the ring on Fleur's finger. The music crossfades to the closing sequence of the "Wedding March' and Fleur and Mont turn upstage and exit* C

The music crossfades again to a twenties' jazz recording being played on a gramophone. The Lights change and there is the sound of people chattering and laughing from the room next door

Soames enters C*, glass in hand and thoughtful. A sad figure for such a gay occasion. He moves downstage* C *and sits. He holds up his champagne glass and looks at the contents and then sips it. He remains lost in thought*

Fleur and Michael Mont suddenly enter from R. *They are both still in their wedding clothes. They laugh and are happy*

Fleur There you are, Daddy. Michael and I were looking for you.
Soames Were you? Well as you can see: here I am.
Fleur We thought we'd cut the cake.
Mont And you must be present for that, sir.
Soames (*looking up and smiling*) Of course. In a moment though. In a moment. All that music and energy . . . (*He smiles*) I need a pause to gain my breath. Not as young as I was.

Fleur senses Soames's deeper feelings

Fleur (*quietly to Mont*) Tell everyone I'll be out in a moment, will you, darling?

Mont goes to speak but Fleur places her finger over his lips. Mont looks at Soames as he realizes

Mont Five minutes. (*He kisses her cheek*)

Mont exits

Fleur comes slowly downstage and sits beside her father. Soames looks at her as she takes his hand

Soames You look absolutely beautiful. Have I told you that?
Fleur Yes.

They smile

Soames Good. Will you be happy?
Fleur Of course.
Soames Because ... I cannot help feeling that history might be repeating itself...
Fleur You mean Irene?
Soames I mean everyone should marry for love. Don't you think? Or have I learnt that too late in life?
Fleur Oh, Daddy, I do so want you to be happy too.
Soames I am happy. (*He holds up his glass*) To you, my darling. (*He drinks*)

Fleur kisses his cheek

Fleur You seem so lonely these last few weeks.
Soames Nonsense. (*He gets up. Pause*) I see Robin Hill's up for sale.
Fleur Yes.
Soames Oh? When did you know?
Fleur The other day when I was passing...
Soames Passing? Richmond?

They look at each other

Oh, my dear ... my dearest...
Fleur (*turning away tearfully*) I received a letter this morning. From Jon.
Soames Where is he?
Fleur British Columbia. He's gone there to farm. He says he's not coming back to England—ever.

They are silent for a moment

Soames Fleur?
Fleur It's all right, Daddy.
Soames (*moving to her*) Are you sure?
Fleur (*turning*) I'm a Forsyte, aren't I?

Soames takes out his handkerchief and wipes the tears from her cheeks

Michael wants me. That's the main thing. And I shall forget Jon, I suppose. If I fly fast and far enough. (*She looks at him and smiles*)
Soames Yes.
Fleur June said something to me before the wedding.
Soames I've finally come to admire that lady. She has a great capacity for forgiveness.
Fleur She said, "we can't control life but we can fight it. Make the best of

things," she said. "I've had to. And look at me." (*She smiles again. With false gaiety*) I'll give you two minutes. Then we'll cut the cake.

Fleur hurries off

Soames moves downstage C *and looks straight out thoughtfully*

Soames My dear, dear Irene ... How you've affected our lives ... If ... If only ... (*The words are left to hang*)

The Lights fade slowly to a Black-out

CURTAIN

FURNITURE AND PROPERTY LIST

ACT 1

On stage: 2 cane tables. *On one:* tray with 7 glasses of champagne (for **Company**)
6 cane chairs
Cane settee C
Various indoor plants: palms, aspidistras, ferns, etc.
Bottle of champagne (for **Servant**)

Off stage: Several folded drawings (**Bosinney**)
Tray with pot of tea, jug of milk, cups, saucers, etc. (**Irene**)
Hat (**Irene**)
Book (**Jo**)
Tray with pot of tea, jug of milk, cups, saucers, etc. (**Servant**)
Small bunch of violets (**Irene**)
Handkerchief (**Jo**)
Tray with cakes, sandwiches, teapot, jug of milk, cups, saucers, etc. (**Servant**)

Personal: **June:** handkerchief
Soames: green moroccan case containing brooch

ACT II

Strike: Tea tray and contents
Cane settee

Set: Sculpture of a head and shoulders on R table
Circular seat

Off stage: Catalogue (**Irene**)
Glass of champagne (**Soames**)

Personal: **Jo:** letter, envelope in pocket
Fleur: handkerchief
Soames: business card, torn letter in pocket, handkerchief
Mont: wedding ring in pocket

LIGHTING PLOT

Property fittings required: nil

ACT I

To open: Full, general lighting

Cue 1	The others turn and watch **Bosinney** and **Irene** *Fade to half. When ready, bring up full lighting* R	(Page 6)
Cue 2	**Soames:** "Build me your palace!" *Fade to black-out. When ready, bring up full lighting* R	(Page 12)
Cue 3	**James** exits *Fade to half. When ready, bring up lighting* R	(Page 15)
Cue 4	**Soames** storms out *Fade to black-out. When ready, fade up full lighting* C	(Page 18)
Cue 5	**Jo** leaves *Fade to half. When ready, bring up full lighting* R	(Page 20)
Cue 6	**Soames:** "Soames is acting at last!" *Fade to half. When ready, bring up rippling firelight effect on* **Soames** DR	(Page 23)
Cue 7	Barrel organ rises to a crescendo *Quick fade to black-out. When ready, bring up full lighting* R	(Page 24)
Cue 8	**Soames** is left alone *Fade to black-out. When ready, bring up lighting* C	(Page 25)
Cue 9	**June** sits sobbing *Fade to black-out. When ready, bring up lighting* R	(Page 27)
Cue 10	**Jo:** "Good-night." *Fade to half. When ready bring up full lighting* R	(Page 28)
Cue 11	Everyone freezes *Crossfade to spotlight* C	(Page 32)
Cue 12	**Irene:** "And does she know he's still married?" *Crossfade to full lighting* R	(Page 33)
Cue 13	**Soames** turns and walks straight out *Fade to black-out*	(Page 36)

ACT II

To open: Full lighting R

Cue 14	**Aunt Hester:** "... this squalid and acrimonious affair." *Crossfade to a spot* L	(Page 38)

Cue 15	**Irene:** "If you want me . . . I am here." *Crossfade to full lighting* R	(Page 39)
Cue 16	**Annette:** ". . . I believe we shall have a daughter." *Black-out. When ready, bring up full, general lighting*	(Page 42)
Cue 17	**Jon:** ". . . I don't think he liked me." *Fade to half* L	(Page 46)
Cue 18	**Jo:** ". . . against a mother's instinct?" *Crossfade to full lighting* C	(Page 48)
Cue 19	**Fleur** and **Jon** smile. They freeze *Crossfade to* R	(Page 49)
Cue 20	**Soames** stalks out. **Annette** freezes *Crossfade to* C	(Page 50)
Cue 21	**Fleur** and **Jon** kiss. They freeze *Crossfade to* L	(Page 51)
Cue 22	**Soames** leaves. **Irene** freezes *Crossfade to* C	(Pagc 53)
Cue 23	**Fleur:** "It's started then." *Fade to half. When ready, bring up full lighting* R	(Page 54)
Cue 24	**Soames:** "Only for the next six weeks, no doubt!" *Crossfade to* L	(Page 56)
Cue 25	**Jon:** ". . . madly in love with you." *Fade to half. When ready, bring up bright moonight effect* L	(Page 57)
Cue 26	**Jo:** "I love you, dear, dear Irene." *Crossfade to full lighting* R	(Page 59)
Cue 27	**Annette** exits *Crossfade to* L	(Page 62)
Cue 28	**Jo:** ". . . so it's to be like this, is it?" *Slow fade to black-out. When ready, bring up full lighting* L	(Page 64)
Cue 29	**Soames** exits *Fade to black-out*	(Page 66)
Cue 30	The "Wedding March" plays *Slowly bring up spot* C	(Page 66)
Cue 31	**Fleur** and **Mont** exit C *Crossfade to full lighting*	(Page 66)
Cue 32	**Soames:** ". . . If . . . If only . . ." *Slow fade to black-out*	(Page 68)

EFFECTS PLOT

ACT I

Cue 1	As the Lights fade to half *Piano music to cover scene change*	(Page 7)
Cue 2	As the Lights fade to half *Piano music for scene change, crossfading into barrel organ effect from outside*	(Page 23)
Cue 3	**Irene** struggles violently *Barrel organ rises to a crescendo and then suddenly stops*	(Page 24)
Cue 4	**June** sits twisting her handkerchief *Door bangs off*	(Page 25)
Cue 5	**June:** "Irene! Irene!" *Door bangs off*	(Page 27)

ACT II

Cue 6	Black-out *Twenties' style piano music for scene change*	(Page 42)
Cue 7	To open SCENE 4 *Birdsong. Continue*	(Page 48)
Cue 8	**Fleur** and **Jon** smile. They freeze *Cut birdsong*	(Page 49)
Cue 9	**Soames** stalks out. **Annette** freezes *Birdsong. Continue*	(Page 50)
Cue 10	**Fleur** and **Jon** kiss. They freeze *Cut birdsong*	(Page 51)
Cue 11	**Soames** leaves. **Irene** freezes *Birdsong. Continue*	(Page 53)
Cue 12	**Fleur:** "It's started, then." *Cut birdsong*	(Page 54)
Cue 13	**Jo:** ". . . so it's to be like this, is it?" *Sombre music for scene change*	(Page 64)
Cue 14	To open SCENE 11 *"Wedding March" plays*	(Page 66)
Cue 15	**Mont** places the ring on **Fleur**'s finger *Crossfade to "Wedding March" closing sequence*	(Page 66)
Cue 16	**Fleur** and **Mont** exit C *Crossfade to twenties' jazz recording being played on a gramophone; bring up sound of people chattering and laughing outside*	(Page 66)

PRINTED IN GREAT BRITAIN
BY BLACK BEAR PRESS LTD
CAMBRIDGE